At Issue

| User-Generated Content

Other Books in the At Issue Series:

At Issue

| User-Generated Content

Roman Espejo, Book Editor

GREENHAVEN PRESS

An imprint of Thomson Gale, a part of The Thomson Corporation

Detroit • New York • San Francisco • New Haven, Conn. • Waterville, Maine • London

Christine Nasso, *Publisher*
Elizabeth Des Chenes, *Managing Editor*

© 2007 The Gale Group.

Star logo is a trademark and Gale and Greenhaven Press are registered trademarks used herein under license.

For more information, contact:
Greenhaven Press
27500 Drake Rd.
Farmington Hills, MI 48331-3535
Or you can visit our Internet site at http://www.gale.com

Articles in Greenhaven Press anthologies are often edited for length to meet page requirements. In addition, original titles of these works are changed to clearly present the main thesis and to explicitly indicate the author's opinion. Every effort is made to ensure that Greenhaven Press accurately reflects the original intent of the authors. Every effort has been made to trace the owners of copyrighted material.

LIBRARY OF CONGRESS CATALOGING-IN-PUBLICATION DATA

User-generated content / Roman Espejo, book editor.
    p. cm. -- (At issue)
    Includes bibliographical references and index.
    ISBN-13: 978-0-7377-3886-5 (hardcover)
    ISBN-13: 978-0-7377-3887-2 (pbk.)
    1. User-generated content. I. Espejo, Roman, 1977-
    ZA4482.U84 2008
    006.7--dc22

                                 2007028822

ISBN-10: 0-7377-3886-3 (hardcover)
ISBN-10: 0-7377-3887-1 (pbk.)

Printed in the United States of America
10 9 8 7 6 5 4 3 2 1

Contents

Introduction

On the cover of its December 25, 2006 issue, *Time* magazine declares that its Person of the Year, which previously included president George W. Bush and Queen Elizabeth II, is "You." Its subhead states, "Yes, you. You control the Information Age. Welcome to your world." Pictured is a computer, its screen specially treated to reflect the reader's face like a mirror.

Time's choice for Person of the Year was a resounding recall of the headlines of 2006, which championed the emerging, innovative ways millions of people started using the Internet and its new technologies. For instance, after Wikipedia was deemed as accurate as *Encyclopedia Britannica* by the scientific journal *Nature* in December 2005, Wikipedia entered the new year as the most popular online encyclopedia by far. During the summer of 2006, within a year and a half of its launch, the video sharing platform YouTube went from being an unknown technology start-up to a worldwide phenomenon. In addition, that August, the social networking giant MySpace reached an astonishing 100 million user accounts. What these Web sites have in common is that their content— digital videos and photographs, podcasts, blogs, and articles—is primarily created by its users. This type of media content is widely known as user-generated content.

The term "user-generated content" came into popular usage in 2005, first among new media and online publishing professionals. Nonetheless, it remains a topic of debate among traditional and new media circles as being a misleading and inadequate description. For example, Scott Karp, managing director at the publishing company Atlantic Media, alleges that most user-generated content is "user-appropriated content," or copyrighted content created by other parties. Karp also argues that the hype surrounding "content created by people" creates an illogical and absurd difference from content "created by journalists and other non-people." Furthermore, designer and blogger Derek Powazek claims that user-generated content consists of "words creepy marketers use" that "imply something to be commodified, harvested, taken advantage of." In fact, Powazek asserts user-generated content is nothing new: "Those people posting to Amazon pages? They're writing *reviews*. Those folks on Flickr? They're taking *photographs*." Therefore, he suggests that the phrase "authentic media" be used instead:

> Authentic media comes to you unfiltered by the global brands and conglomerates that have taken over the mainstream media. Authentic media is the raw, first-person narrative you can find on blogs and home pages. Authentic media is what happens when the mediators get out of the way and give the mic over to the people who actually have something to say. The best part about this phrase? It paints the rest of the mediascape as inauthentic. I can live with that.

On the contrary, technology expert and blogger Debi Jones contends that the phrase "authentic media" is as problematic as "user-generated content" because "many independent creators would prefer that corporate media become more participatory and we can't gain their cooperation through alienation or demeaning their products by calling them inauthentic." Jones asks, "What label creates a distinction between independent and corporate produced media?" and lists, but does not promote, other terms, including "participatory media," "citizens' journalism," and "media 2.0."

Yet other technology and media professionals, such as Solomon Rothman, chief information officer at Web development firm Social Media Systems, believe that using the term "user-generated content" to describe amateur digital videos and photographs, podcasts, blogs, and other works "correctly portrays a strong idea and is a positive ideology behind the changing world of new media." Rothman proposes that "while you're consuming a resource and contributing to it, you're producing user-generated content," and it is "an easy-to-understand term and one that works so well."

The discussion and debate surrounding user-generated content highlights the issues arising with this new classification of content in the mainstream media—from the legal implications and licensing battles regarding fair use and copyright infringement of content being shared on YouTube, to defining the ethical responsibilities of bloggers within the field of journalism. The authors in *At Issue: User-Generated Content* explore these and other topics, which impact the lives of people who uphold that they are affected, empowered, or compromised by the rapidly evolving Internet.

1

User-Generated Content: An Overview

John Lanchester

John Lanchester is a British novelist, journalist, and a contributing editor to the London Review of Books.

The Internet is in the midst of another revolution—this time, it's in the hands of the millions of people sitting in front of computer screens networking, collaborating, and sharing with each other. Their on-line profiles, photo albums, journals, and Web logs (or blogs) are collectively known as user-generated content. Web sites that make editing, organizing, collecting, and sharing these creations easier, such as MySpace, YouTube, and Wikipedia, have skyrocketed in popularity. Not everyone believes that such sites truly connect people, but it is undeniable that the Internet has become a commonplace presence like many of the technologies that have come before it.

In July 2005 [media executive] Rupert Murdoch had what was widely seen as a brain-fart. He spent $580m [million] on an Internet company that was only two years old. The company was called MySpace, and it was the fastest-growing new example of what are called "social networking" sites: a place where young people can post pictures of themselves, solicit friends to get in touch, let people listen to their music, answer pointless questionnaires, and in general go on at great length about the favourite subject of every young person on the planet: themselves. The company was seen as a fad by the few grown-ups who knew about it, and was notorious among geeks for its horribly irregular site design. It had no revenue stream to speak of. The "business model" for the company— the way it was eventually going to make money—was . . . er . . . next question. There was widespread tittering. Murdoch, who lost a lot of money on the first cycle of Internet hype, had bought another pup.

In August [2006], MySpace, which on various measures is now the busiest Internet site in the world, signed a deal with Google guaranteeing it $900m [million] in search-related advertising revenue over the next four years. Murdoch has made some big mistakes with his big bets, but MySpace isn't one of them. Instead, it is the exemplar of a new wave of innovation on the Internet, an innovation focused not so much on new technology as on the way people are beginning to use existing technology. It is, I think, significant that the co-founder of MySpace, Tom Anderson, is what used to be a rarity in the net world, an arts graduate, with, instead of the computer science PhD that would once have been de rigueur, an MA in, of all things, film criticism. . . .

It is when people stop thinking of something as a piece of technology that the thing starts to have its biggest impact. Wheels, wells, books, spectacles were all once wonders of the world; now they are everywhere, and we can't live without them. The Internet hasn't quite got to that point, but it is getting there. . . .

Wireless modems, and the omnipresent Internet they permit—the Internet that is everywhere, like the air—still seem miraculous to me, but to 10-year-olds they seem utterly prosaic.

Growing Up with the Internet

People are growing up with the Internet, and the Internet is growing up with them. It is evolving. Email was once a marvel of practicality and utility; people under the age of 25, though, never knew a time before it was broken by spam, and prefer to use instant messaging or texting. In the corporate world, as a publisher once told me, "email's main function is as an instrument of torture". In civilian life, I increasingly notice that people don't actually read their email; they sort of skim it, and get the gist, and any fine distinctions or crucial information are usually best communicated in some other way. So the heroic period of email is already in the past. No one could have predicted that, just as no one could have predicted the extraordinary, dizzying multiplying of the number of blogs being written. (I don't say read.) That number has been doubling every six months for the past three years: there are now, as of July 31, [2005,] more than 50m [million] blogs on the Internet; 175,000 new blogs are created every day—that's two every second. The dominant languages (they jockey from month to month) are Chinese, Japanese and English. There are 1.6m [million] blog posts a day.

What does that mean? What should we think about it? It's hard to know where to start, other than to say that those figures are from Technorati, a blog-tracking and searching website that is one of the indispensable sites for anyone with an interest in the net. What is a typical blog? Who knows? Somebody wittering about what they had for breakfast, or complaining about their boyfriend, or posting terrible photographs of their dog, or how they played Pong last night and it was more fun than some of their new games, or how lousy it is being a policeman. . . . It's almost impossible to think of a subject that isn't being blogged about.

The Internet is no longer about corporations telling you what to do think or buy; it's about things people create.

The shorthand term for what is happening now is "Web 2.0", a designation coined at a conference in 2004 by the web-business booster Tim O'Reilly, as describing "an attitude rather than a technology". The phrase is a shorthand for the second Internet goldrush, to follow the one that ended in 2000 with arguably the biggest destruction of investors' capital in history. From the business point of view, the defining feature of this new goldrush is that established companies are throwing huge amounts of money at upstarts who have three things in common: they have grown from nowhere with astonishing speed; they have no revenue stream to speak of; and most of their content is provided by their users. Thus we have Murdoch's buy of MySpace in July 2005, Yahoo's of Flickr in March 2005 and its rumoured to be imminent buy of Facebook for around $1bn [billion], and—in money terms the biggest of them all—Google's $1.6bn acquisition of YouTube on October 9 [2006]. That's a great deal of money raining down on some happy, happy nerds. Chad Hurley and Steve Chen only founded YouTube in February 2005. Their creation has grown in value at a rate of more than $100m a month—which must surely be a world record. That's a hell of a lot of money to be earned by the founders of a company with no earnings.

An Approach to Creating Things

What all these new kind of sites share is an approach to creating things: "user-created content", in the jargon. The Internet is no longer about corporations telling you what to do, think or buy; it's about things people create. The stuff they create falls into two very broad types. (The types aren't distinct; they blur and overlap and mash-up, as is the new way of it.)

The first type is the collective or collaborative gathering of information. One of the most important examples of this came in the wake of Hurricane Katrina, when survivors were dispersed all over the place, information was chaotic and contradictory, and the government, temporarily, seemed to collapse. A group of net-heads, led by a hacker called David Geilhufe, realised that scattered information was being posted to blogs and news sites, and put together a team of thousands of volunteers to "screenscrape" this information off the net and amalgamate it in one place: *Katrinalist.net*, which within a single day had collated information about 50,000 survivors of the disaster. No other medium could have done that, and no government agency came close to having the nous [intellect].

The collaborative aspects of the net have tremendous power to gather and collate information. Wikipedia is one example of this: the biggest and fastest-growing encyclopedia on the net, and the subject of many horror stories on the part of what bloggers like to call the MSM (that's mainstream media, like this). Wikipedia-bashing is all the rage in the press, and there's no denying the encyclopedia's flaws; but it's also a reference resource of extraordinary range and ease of access and, when the subject involved is sufficiently uncontroversial, remarkable usefulness. The rule of thumb with Wikipedia is that the more nerds argue about an entry, the less useful it is. (Incidentally, in the American university system, any use of Wikipedia immediately guarantees the student an F.)

Another collective site—one I look at every day—is Digg, in which users click on a thumbs-up to vote for interesting stories. Digg, Wikipedia and comparable sites have just been the subject of a blistering essay by Jaron Lanier, a scientist-thinker-mountebank who invented the term "virtual reality" and whose essay in *Edge*, an online magazine, complains about "Digital Maoism" and the tendency of these sites to form a "hive mind", a collective, consensus reality. And there's something in that: in any arena of human activity, you don't get a spiky, idiosyncratic take on things from sites where people vote for the most popular anything. But you do get a sense of what people find interesting, what they're reading about and talking about; a lot of what is on there is interesting and funny, and anything boring and/or stupid can be quickly scanned and rejected. The ease and speed of not-reading is one of the good things about reading on the net.

Me Media

If collective sites are one of the big categories of New Thing, the other is to do with personal sites—what have been called "Me Media". But the distinctions are not clear-cut, and some interesting things happen in the overlap. Del.icio.us is a bookmark site where people list favourite places on the web—sites, blogs or whatever—which makes it a personal thing, but the entries can be tagged (ie, they can have subject labels attached) by anyone who looks at them. This gives Del.icio.us a flavour that is both personal and collective: it's about individual likes, as viewed in a group perspective, or something. I find I use it most when something else on the net sends me there, and I become curious about what someone who's interested in the same things as me finds interesting. Flickr is another site in this personal/collective overlap. It's a place where people post and tag photographs, often with multiple categories: so, say, a photo of a woman in a bikini on a beach in Brazil might be tagged as "beach", "bikini", "Brazil", and "whoa baby". I don't fully understand why people are so keen to post private photographs to Flickr, or why people are so keen to look at other people's photographs, but that's just me. Millions do.

YouTube is a hugely popular site that is more firmly in the personal category. It is basically a huge clearing house where people can post videos of, well, of anything. Want to film yourself standing on one leg, and let strangers see the result? YouTube! Then everyone who views it can vote on its popularity—that's the collective touch. Quite a lot of YouTube is pilfered off the TV: the point at which the site became a household name in the US was when it rebroadcast a sketch called Lazy Sunday from Saturday Night Live. NBC forced them to take the footage down, but the resulting publicity turned YouTube from a geek favourite to a general favourite. Because anybody can put anything (except porn) on to YouTube, I'd say roughly 98% of it is so boring that it rivals prescription sleeping aids, but the other 2% still adds up to a lot of stuff. At the time of writing, the most popular thing on YouTube is Peter, a 79-year-old man from Norfolk, complaining about modern life. His unique selling point is that he is the oldest person on YouTube. Peter is like a nicer, duller, less funny, less incisive version of Victor Meldrew [a character on British television]. People love him.

We are now firmly in the category of the personal site. One way of putting it is to say that collective sites are useful (except when they're not) and personal sites are interesting (except when they're not). The big daddy of these, the 900lb gorilla, the Godzilla, the current Biggest of Big Things, is MySpace. Readers of the business pages first heard of MySpace when Murdoch bought it in 2005, and the site forced itself into the consciousness of the wider public over the past year, mainly through the MySpace-powered breakthroughs of three musical acts: Gnarls Barkley, the Arctic Monkeys and Lily Allen.

If you're not on MySpace . . . you don't exist.

That was no accident. Music made MySpace what it is today. At the time the company launched, in 2003, the then biggest social networking site, Friendster, didn't allow bands to promote themselves. The men behind MySpace saw that as a crucial mistake, not least because of music's centrality to young people's self-definition. Bands gave them a reason for visiting MySpace, and something to talk about when they went there. "Music is a major cornerstone of our success," Tom Anderson says today. "We've got over two million bands on the site already and the number just keeps growing. As other artists—comedians, film-makers, designers, etc—have come on the site, the success we've seen with music has repeated itself. If you're connected to culture and offer compelling content, you can reach broad segments of our community pretty fast. That's true if you're Snoop Dogg or an unsigned garage band in Liverpool."

The 10th Biggest Country in the World

Cool—everything to do with cool—is a big, big business. MySpace is in that business. It has more than 110m registered users; if it were a country it would be the 10th biggest in the world, just behind Mexico. Its audience, heavily skewed towards the affluent youth of the west, is a marketer's and advertiser's fantasy. In time, this might be a problem for MySpace, as companies become more astute about how to manipulate the apparent chaos and spontaneity of the site to plant manufactured hype. (There has just been a kerfuffle of this sort on YouTube, about a fake video blog called Lonelygirl15.) Chris DeWolfe, the CEO of MySpace, was bullish about this when I asked him. "I'm not sure how anyone could falsely construct hype on MySpace," he said, "since the community rejects pretty much anything that isn't authentic." Well, quite—and they might decide that MySpace itself is not wholly authentic. But although there are murmurings about hype, for now, the site is riding high. "If you're not on MySpace," an American teenager told a researcher, "you don't exist."

The hardest thing to get your head around is the sheer size of this audience. When you first browse MySpace pages, the site asks what country you're interested in, which gender, what age range, and whether you want only to see people who've posted photographs of themselves. If you leave all of those settings on the default options, you are taken to see the MySpace pages of women in Afghanistan between 18 and 35 who have posted pictures of themselves. Guess how many there are? Three thousand. I thought that was a mistake—what, 3,000 women peering out from beneath their burkhas in Kabul to post complaints about their mothers-in-law?—but when I started clicking, I landed first on the page of a 18-year-old woman who is a private in the US army and based at Bagram. That's when I realised that most of these pages belong to young women soldiers, and also what MySpace is: a place where you can go to communicate with, if not quite anyone in the world, then with an 18-year-old US army private who likes Sixpence None The Richer, Eagle Eye Cherry and the Ramones, has a weakness for deli pickles, a fear of snakes and whose ambition for this year is to achieve abs of steel. And there are 100m more pages where that one came from.

There is something freaking-out about this. It's hard to know what to think of a phenomenon where quite so many people are so on display, so contactable, so ready to be got in touch with, so connected. Speaking for myself, I feel a strong sense of intrusiveness when I look at people's MySpace pages—a reaction that makes no sense at all, since the whole point of these pages is that they've been designed to be looked at. While I've been working on this piece, I've been showing MySpace to people who don't know it and asking what they think of it, what it reminds them of. One of the best answers was given by my wife, who said it reminded her of scrapbooks, the kind that teenagers used to keep—postcards, photos, lists of likes and dislikes, doodles, best friends, boyfriends, crushed flowers, crushes. But while all that is true, the truest thing is to say that you can't really come up with a metaphor for MySpace. It really is a new thing. . . .

Connectedness and Separation

MySpace is all about connectedness; but equally, and perhaps more truthfully, it could be said that it's all about separation. In 2000 a man called Mitch Maddox changed his name by deed poll to Dotcomguy and lived for a year without going out of his house: all his shopping, all his everything, was done exclusively over the Internet. That was a stunt, obviously—a rather depressing stunt—but it made the point that this is what the world is now like. (In case you're worried, he changed his name back to Mitch Maddox at the end of the year.) You can make your living, do your shopping, pay your taxes, enjoy your entertainments, have friends and relationships, all without going out of your house, or indeed without moving away from your computer screen except to go to the fridge and toilet. Now that, it seems to me, is a profoundly grim thought.

Everyone sitting at a computer screen, increasingly, wants everything to be all about them.

Tom Anderson doesn't agree. "For most of our users," he told me, "the vast majority of their MySpace friends are also offline friends. They're just connecting through a different medium when they're on MySpace. The connection between someone in Leeds and a comedian in Los Angeles would probably never happen if it weren't for MySpace, so it enables friendship and connection far more than it limits it." Pressing the point, I asked if the MySpace idea of a friend represented a devaluation of the idea of friendship. Again, he didn't agree. "It's pretty cool when you can connect directly with your neighbour and the Black Eyed Peas at the same time. MySpace gives our members the ability to reach such an incredible range of people and have direct contact with them. I'm not sure how that devalues friendship so much as it expands the range of potential friends you can have."

Well, maybe. About five years ago I was checking my email in a cybercafe in Sydney. Being nosey, I began sneaking discreet peeks at my neighbours' computer screens. On my left, an American backpacker was writing to a man she'd met in India, debating whether they should arrange to meet again and take their relationship further or whether they should leave it as it was, as a Bogart-and-Bergman we'll-always-have-Dharamsala memory. On my right, a man in a turban was writing to a woman not his wife about how his wife did not understand him. It struck me that everybody on the net is sitting alone at a computer screen, and many of them are wishing they weren't alone, while also, often, in some deep way, preferring that they are alone and being nervous of the alternative. Sit someone at a computer screen and let it sink in that they are fully, definitively alone; then watch what happens. They will reach out for other people; but only part of the way. They will have "friends", which are not the same thing as friends, and a lively online life, which is not the same thing as a social life; they will feel more connected, but they will be just as alone. Everybody sitting at a computer screen is alone. Everybody sitting at a computer screen is at the centre of the world. Everybody sitting at a computer screen, increasingly, wants everything to be all about them. This is our first glimpse of what people who grow up with the net will want from the net. One of the cleverest things about MySpace is the name.

2

User-Generated Content Can Be Useful to Mainstream Media

Deloitte

Deloitte is a multinational business and financial advisory firm headquartered in Wilton, Connecticut.

Because of the success of YouTube, the growing eminence of blogging, and the wave of citizen journalism, user-generated content has been positioned as the downfall of established media. For the most part, however, the quality of user-generated content is unlikely to surpass the output of the established media. In addition, companies could use social networking sites and online forums to generate publicity and talent searching. Finally, though the number of "new media" viewers and enthusiasts is rapidly rising, it cannot be compared to "old media" such as television and radio, as there are fundamental differences between Internet-based and analog formats.

Digital user-generated content has been cast as the eventual conqueror of the established media world. Blogs could batter established media empire. Citizen journalists may render the professional columnist redundant. Amateur filmmakers, armed with camera phones, could even topple Hollywood.

This view has been gathering steam during 2006 and may become even more prevalent in 2007, as the volume of blogs

Deloitte, "Media Predictions: TMT Trends 2007," January 2007, pp. 6, 13. Deloitte & Touche USA LLP. Reproduced by permission.

grows, the specification of mobile phones improves and the number of websites supporting user-generated content rises.

Yet the majority of user-generated content is likely to remain mediocre, and thus of little interest or value to most. Essentially it is not likely to pose a major threat to the media industry.

In 2007 the majority of blogs and bloggers, while being available to the billion Internet users around the world, may well find themselves ignored by most of that number. While a few thousand blogs may attract significant traffic, few of the estimated 60 million bloggers, excepting those columnists who have just rebranded themselves as such, may be able to make a living from their weblogs alone. . . . In 2007 the role of the individual with a camera phone may be recognized as being more like that of a digital eyewitness, providing a photographic or video-based comment on an emerging news story, rather than a journalist trained to analyze and interpret an unfolding event. Websites whose original ethos was to collect user-generated content may find their most popular content is user selected rather then user created.

Indeed in 2007, as in years to come, owning a professional-quality video camera, a PC or a mobile phone is unlikely magically to imbue the majority of people with talent, much as it is improbable that a paintbrush could produce a budding Picasso. In many cases, user-generated content may increasingly be seen as a vindication of, rather than an assault on, the professional media industry.

However, this does not mean that digital, user-generated content has no role in the professional media world. Indeed in 2007 all forms of user-generated content should complement established media, perhaps to an extent that has never been seen before. As well as readers' letters, listeners' phone calls and children's drawings continuing to feed into newspapers, radio shows and television programs, respectively, their digital equivalents are also likely to be used in a similar way—to complement professional content.

Further, digital, user-generated views may well be used to provide informal feedback on a wide range of media, and websites featuring user-generated opinions and recommendations may also be used, subsequently or openly, as an increasingly important research and marketing channel.

Making User-generated Content Meaningful

In 2007, digital, user-generated content may offer more of an opportunity than a threat to incumbent media companies. The more media companies take an opportunistic stance towards user-generated content, the more they are likely to be able to exploit its potential value. The industry should consider, for example, how such content can be incorporated into traditional media formats.

For user-generated content to be meaningful, clearly it has to generate revenue, directly or indirectly. While using the public's content for program and new concept creation can generate revenues, that opportunity is likely to be limited.

More broadly however, the established media sector could grow its top line by using user-generated content channels to raise awareness of existing, forthcoming and archive material, grow market share, engender loyalty and, indeed, identify new talent.

A media company could publicize a new media property by creating a buzz in social networking sites and virtual worlds. Music companies have used social networks to raise the profile of emerging acts, some established bands have attempted to maintain profile by playing concerts in virtual worlds. They could also use user-generated content as a means of gaging reaction to established content, from television shows to newspaper columns. Companies could either analyze discussions on Internet forums or ask consumers directly to review new movies, plays and restaurants, rather than just rely on the opinions of professional journalists. This approach could create a more interactive and intimate relationship with customers.

Headlines about new media's near vertical rise abound. Analyses of the travails of old media are similarly plentiful. Yet terms of reference often differ and context is sadly lacking.

Digital, user-generated content could be used to enhance the loyalty of an established media format, such as a television show based on viewers videos. The broadcast show could feature a selection of the producer's picks, the best of the rest could then be made available online for viewing and rating. The most popular of the Web-based videos could then be broadcast on the following week's show. This approach could both retain interest in the show and add viewing hours, drawing the locus of eyeballs away from the PC and back to the television.

New media companies could also use digital, user-generated content as a means of establishing new content. Thus the A&R [artist and repertoire] function of music companies, or the talent-scouting unit of a movie studio could partly move online. However media companies should recognize that online searchers for talent can be just as arduous and painstaking as the physical quest.

Analog Apples and Digital Oranges

Headlines about new media's near vertical rise abound. Analyses of the travails of old media are similarly plentiful. Yet terms of reference often differ and context is sadly lacking. This causes misunderstandings that are likely to linger throughout 2007.

The success of 2006's new media darling, social networking, is often expressed in terms of daily downloads and unique viewers. Though the numbers are enormous, they are perhaps deceivingly impressive. YouTube, one of the largest social networking sites, has been positioned as a threat to the traditional television industry. YouTube's users both upload and download, in far greater numbers than watch television, short videos that some regard as a directly comparable alternative. YouTube enjoys over 100 million downloads every day and boasts 70 million monthly unique users. During the course of 2007, these numbers may well rise, perhaps significantly.

So how does YouTube fare, when compared with one traditional television broadcaster, the BBC, in the context of one nation, the United Kingdom? BBC's four terrestrial television stations now consider a prime-time, weekend audience of 10 million viewers, from a population of 60 million, a major success. But a television viewer is not directly comparable to a unique viewer on the Internet, and a television program is quite different to a video clip. The former is longer, and generally has higher production values. The average length of the 20 most viewed video clips to date on YouTube is a shade over three minutes, the overall limit is 10 minutes. A television program often lasts 30 minutes, sometimes more.

And if we compare total hours watched, a quite different picture emerges. The number of hours watched of the BBC's television output in the United Kingdom alone, far outstrips that of YouTube globally, by a ratio of 10 to one. And that does not include the growing number of hours of BBC television watched over the Internet.

Tapping Into New Media's Potential

Media companies, advertisers and even telecommunications operators have been keen to tap into new media's potential. In 2007 they should continue to do so, but ideally when informed by using only statistics that are directly comparable.

Balanced, comparable statistics that clearly show the relative performance of all types of media, both old and new should ensure that investors' expectations are properly managed, that advertisers' budgets are appropriately allocated, and that acquisitions are accurately priced.

Any company considering new media applications should always consider the total addressable market. For new media that is likely to be limited initially by the number of broadband connected PCs and mobile phones. While over a billion PCs are forecast to be in use in 2007, only a quarter are expected to be connected via broadband. As for mobile, of over 2.1 billion mobile phones that are in use globally, only 282 million are capable of handling new media content and services, and an even smaller percentage are actually used to access them.

In contrast, penetration of television and radio is almost guaranteed to remain several orders of magnitude higher, both in 2007 and for several years to come. In 2007 there should be some 1.7 billion televisions in use, with sales running at over 160 million each year, and more than 2.2 billion radio sets in use.

3

Wikipedia's Accuracy Is Comparable to Britannica

Daniel Terdiman

Daniel Terdiman is a staff writer for CNET News.com.

User-generated content is responsible for the phenomenal growth of Wikipedia, the on-line encyclopedia. Thousands of users, from casual readers to experts, contribute to and edit Wikipedia's mounting number of entries. Critics of Wikipedia argue that because anyone can add a change or revise a Wikipedia entry, it cannot compete with the academic integrity of Encyclopedia Britannica, which relies on paid professionals and experts to produce their entries. However, a study Nature *conducted shows that, on average, Wikipedia and Britannica articles are comparable in their frequency of errors. Greater oversight from scientists, researchers, and other experts can enhance Wikipedia's accuracy even more.*

Wikipedia is about as good a source of accurate information as Britannica, the venerable [respected] standard-bearer of facts about the world around us, according to a study published [in 2005] in the [science] journal *Nature*.

Wikipedia's Past Problems

Wikipedia, the free, open-access encyclopedia, has taken a great deal of flak in the press for problems related to the credibility of its authors and its general accountability.

Daniel Terdiman, "Study: Wikipedia as Accurate as Britannica," CNET News.com, December 15, 2005. Reproduced by permission.

In particular, Wikipedia has taken hits for its inclusion, for four months, of an anonymously written article linking former journalist John Seigenthaler to the assassinations of Robert Kennedy [U.S. Attorney General and Senator] and John F. Kennedy [the 35th U.S. President]. At the same time, the blogosphere was buzzing for several days about podcasting pioneer Adam Curry's being accused of anonymously deleting references to others' seminal work on the technology.

In response to situations like these and others in its history, Wikipedia founder Jimmy Wales has always maintained that the service and its community are built around a self-policing and self-cleaning nature that is supposed to ensure its articles are accurate.

Still, many critics have tried to downplay its role as a source of valid information and have often pointed to the Encyclopedia Britannica as an example of an accurate reference.

Testing Validity

For its study, *Nature* chose articles from both sites in a wide range of topics and sent them to what it called "relevant" field experts for peer review. The experts then compared the competing articles—one from each site on a given topic—side by side, but were not told which article came from which site. *Nature* got back 42 usable reviews from its field of experts.

In the end, the journal found just eight serious errors, such as general misunderstandings of vital concepts, in the articles. Of those, four came from each site. They did, however, discover a series of factual errors, omissions or misleading statements. All told, Wikipedia had 162 such problems, while Britannica had 123.

That averages out to 2.92 mistakes per article for Britannica and 3.86 for Wikipedia.

"An expert-led investigation carried out by *Nature*—the first to use peer review to compare Wikipedia and Britannica's coverage of science," the journal wrote, "suggests that such high-profile examples (like the Seigenthaler and Curry situations) are the exception rather than the rule."

Wikipedia Pleased with Results

And to Wales, while Britannica came out looking a little bit more accurate than Wikipedia, the *Nature* study was validation of his service's fundamental structure.

"I was very pleased, just to see that (the study) was reasonably favorable," Wales told CNET News.com. "I think it provides, for us, a great counterpoint to the press coverage we've gotten recently, because it puts the focus on the broader quality and not just one article."

He also acknowledged that the error rate for each encyclopedia was not insignificant, and added that he thinks such numbers demonstrate that broad review of encyclopedia articles is needed.

He also said that the results belie [contradict] the notion that Britannica is infallible [incapable of error].

"I have very great respect for Britannica," Wales said. But "I think there is a general view among a lot of people that it has no errors, like, 'I read it in Britannica, it must be true.' It's good that people see that there are a lot of errors everywhere."

Britannica Reacts

To Britannica officials, however, the *Nature* results showed that Wikipedia still has a way to go.

"The (*Nature*) article is saying that Wikipedia has a third more errors" than Britannica, said Jorge Cauz, president of Encyclopedia Britannica.

But Cauz and editor in chief Dale Hoiberg also said they were concerned that *Nature* had not specified the problems that it had found in Britannica.

"We've asked them a number of questions about the process they used," Hoiberg said. "They said in (their article) that the inaccuracies included errors, omissions and misleading statements. But there's no indication of how many of each. So we're very eager to look at that and explore it because we take it very seriously."

4

Wikipedia Is a Flawed Research Tool

John Seigenthaler

John Seigenthaler is a retired journalist and a former editorial page editor at USA TODAY. *He also worked for former U.S. attorney general Robert F. Kennedy in the 1960s. From May 2005 to October 2005, Seigenthaler's Wikipedia biography falsely alleged that he was thought to be involved in both Robert's and John F. Kennedy's assassinations.*

The popular online encyclopedia Wikipedia, which depends on user-generated content for its entries, is a flawed tool for research. Its authors are anonymous and nearly impossible to track; therefore, they are virtually free from liability for providing erroneous or even libelous information. Furthermore, although Wikipedia contributors supposedly assume accountability for inaccuracies that appear in its entries and correct them within minutes, they have allowed a damaging, false allegation to remain in a biography for several months.

> "John Seigenthaler Sr. was the assistant to Attorney General Robert Kennedy in the early 1960's. For a brief time, he was thought to have been directly involved in the Kennedy assassinations of both John, and his brother, Bobby. Nothing was ever proven." —Wikipedia

This is a highly personal story about Internet character assassination. It could be your story.

I have no idea whose sick mind conceived the false, malicious "biography" that appeared under my name for 132 days on Wikipedia, the popular, online, free encyclopedia whose authors are unknown and virtually untraceable. There was more:

"John Seigenthaler moved to the Soviet Union in 1971, and returned to the United States in 1984," Wikipedia said. "He started one of the country's largest public relations firms shortly thereafter."

At age 78 [in 2005], I thought I was beyond surprise or hurt at anything negative said about me. I was wrong. One sentence in the biography was true. I was Robert Kennedy's administrative assistant in the early 1960s. I also was his pall-bearer. It was mind-boggling when my son, John Seigenthaler, journalist with NBC News, phoned later to say he found the same scurrilous text on Reference.com and Answers.com.

I had heard for weeks from teachers, journalists and historians about "the wonderful world of Wikipedia," where millions of people worldwide visit daily for quick reference "facts," composed and posted by people with no special expertise or knowledge—and sometimes by people with malice.

At my request, executives of the three websites now have removed the false content about me. But they don't know, and can't find out, who wrote the toxic sentences.

Anonymous Author

I phoned Jimmy Wales, Wikipedia's founder and asked, "Do you . . . have any way to know who wrote that?"

"No, we don't," he said. Representatives of the other two websites said their computers are programmed to copy data verbatim from Wikipedia, never checking whether it is false or factual.

Naturally, I want to unmask my "biographer." And, I am interested in letting many people know that Wikipedia is a flawed and irresponsible research tool.

But searching cyberspace for the identity of people who post spurious information can be frustrating. I found on

Wikipedia the registered IP (Internet Protocol) number of my "biographer"—65-81-97-208. I traced it to a customer of Bell-South Internet. That company advertises a phone number to report "Abuse Issues." An electronic voice said all complaints must be e-mailed. My two e-mails were answered by identical form letters, advising me that the company would conduct an investigation but might not tell me the results. It was signed "Abuse Team."

Wales, Wikipedia's founder, told me that BellSouth would not be helpful. "We have trouble with people posting abusive things over and over and over," he said. "We block their IP numbers, and they sneak in another way. So we contact the service providers, and they are not very responsive."

For four months, Wikipedia depicted me as a suspected assassin. . . .

After three weeks, hearing nothing further about the Abuse Team investigation, I phoned BellSouth's Atlanta corporate headquarters, which led to conversations between my lawyer and BellSouth's counsel. My only remote chance of getting the name, I learned, was to file a "John or Jane Doe" lawsuit against my "biographer." Major communications Internet companies are bound by federal privacy laws that protect the identity of their customers, even those who defame online. Only if a lawsuit resulted in a court subpoena would Bell-South give up the name.

Little Legal Recourse

Federal law also protects online corporations—BellSouth, AOL, MCI, Wikipedia, etc.—from libel lawsuits. Section 230 of the Communications Decency Act, passed in 1996, specifically states that "no provider or user of an interactive computer service shall be treated as the publisher or speaker." That legalese means that, unlike print and broadcast companies, online service providers cannot be sued for disseminating defamatory attacks on citizens posted by others.

Recent low-profile court decisions document that Congress effectively has barred defamation in cyberspace. Wikipedia's website acknowledges that it is not responsible for inaccurate information, but Wales, in a recent C-Span interview with [C-Span chief executive officer] Brian Lamb, insisted that his website is accountable and that his community of thousands of volunteer editors (he said he has only one paid employee) corrects mistakes within minutes.

My experience refutes that. My "biography" was posted May 26 [2005]. On May 29, one of Wales' volunteers "edited" it only by correcting the misspelling of the word "early." For four months, Wikipedia depicted me as a suspected assassin before Wales erased it from his website's history Oct. 5. The falsehoods remained on Answers.com and Reference.com for three more weeks.

In the C-Span interview, Wales said Wikipedia has "millions" of daily global visitors and is one of the world's busiest websites. His volunteer community runs the Wikipedia operation, he said. He funds his website through a non-profit foundation and estimated a 2006 budget of "about a million dollars."

And so we live in a universe of new media with phenomenal opportunities for worldwide communications and research—but populated by volunteer vandals with poison-pen intellects. Congress has enabled them and protects them.

When I was a child, my mother lectured me on the evils of "gossip." She held a feather pillow and said, "If I tear this open, the feathers will fly to the four winds, and I could never get them back in the pillow. That's how it is when you spread mean things about people."

For me, that pillow is a metaphor for Wikipedia.

5

Blogging Is Important to Journalism

J. D. Lasica

J. D. Lasica is a writer, blogger, and cofounder of Ourmedia.org, a grassroots new media organization.

Critics argue that blogs do not have the credibility of "old-school" and mainstream journalism because bloggers lack the editorial oversight and carefully honed skills of professional journalists. Blogs, however, are becoming a more important part of the complex "media ecosystem." Blogs often inform the mainstream media of important issues and events and continuously report stories that become neglected by major media outlets. Bloggers have prominence and large readerships because of their accurate and relevant writing. Blogging enhances journalism by making journalism more accessible and interactive to audiences.

Suggest to an old-school journalist that Weblogs have anything to do with journalism, and you'll be met with howls of derision. Amateur bloggers typically have no editorial oversight, no training in the craft, and no respect for the news media's rules and standards. Does the free-for-all renegade publishing form known as blogging really have anything to do with journalism?

Well, yes it does.

Consider:

- During the peace demonstrations in February [2003], Lisa Rein took to the streets of San Francisco and Oakland, California, camcorder in hand, and taped video footage of the marchers and speakers, such as Representative Barbara Lee, Harry Belafonte, and antiwar activist Ron Kovic. She posted the video on her Weblog, complete with color commentary, providing much deeper coverage of the events than a viewer would get by watching the local news.

- At technology and media conferences, such as PopTech, South by Southwest, and Digital Hollywood, bloggers in the audience have reported conference events in real time, posting photographs, speaker transcripts, and summaries and analysis of key points a full day before readers could see comparable stories in the daily newspaper.

- On [2003's] Super Bowl Sunday, a 22-year-old blogger in Los Angeles named Jessica Rios braved the freezing cold to attend a televised outdoor concert by the British group Coldplay. She came home and blogged it, giving her take on the concert and reporting the band's play list. Like hundreds of others who watched the show and wanted to learn the names of the songs played, I turned to the Internet. I came up empty when I visited abc.com and coldplay.com. But hundreds of us found them (through Google) on Rios's blog.

Rios probably didn't know it, but she was committing a random act of journalism. And that's the real revolution here: In a world of micro-content delivered to niche audiences, more and more of the small tidbits of news that we encounter each day are being conveyed through personal media—chiefly Weblogs.

Call it participatory journalism or journalism from the edges. Simply put, it refers to individuals playing an active role in the process of collecting, reporting, sorting, analyzing and disseminating news and information—a task once reserved almost exclusively to the news media.

Bloggers value informal conversation, egalitarianism, subjective points of view, and colorful writing over profits, central control, objectivity and filtered prose.

Weblogs are the most popular expression of this new media form. Blogs have exploded in popularity in the past year, fueled by greater access to bandwidth and low-cost, often free software. More than a half million people have taken up the tools of self-publishing to create personal journals on subjects as diverse as politics, microbiology and tropical fish.

"Blogs are in some ways a new form of journalism, open to anyone who can establish and maintain a Web site, and they have exploded in the past year," Walter Mossberg wrote in his *Wall Street Journal* technology column last March. "The good thing about them is that they introduce fresh voices into the national discourse on various topics and help build communities of interest through their collections of links."

Mossberg's description of Weblogs as a new kind of journalism might trouble hidebound journalists. But it is a journalism of a different sort, one not tightly confined by the profession's traditions and values.

Mainstream news operations are businesses supported by advertising. As hierarchical organizations, they value smooth production workflows, profitability and rigorous editorial standards. Weblogs adhere to a different set of values. Bloggers value informal conversation, egalitarianism, subjective points of view, and colorful writing over profits, central control, objectivity and filtered prose.

Clay Shirky, an adjunct professor at New York University who has consulted on the social and economic effects of Internet technologies, sees the difference between traditional media and Weblog communities this way: "The order of things in broadcast is 'filter, then publish.' The order in communities is 'publish, then filter.' If you go to a dinner party, you don't submit your potential comments to the hosts, so that they can tell you which ones are good enough to air before the group, but this is how broadcast works every day. Writers submit their stories in advance, to be edited or rejected before the public ever sees them. Participants in a community, by contrast, say what they have to say, and the good is sorted from the mediocre after the fact."

Creating a New Media Ecosystem

Many traditional journalists are dismissive of bloggers, describing them as self-interested or unskilled amateurs. Conversely, many bloggers look upon mainstream media as an arrogant, elitist club that puts its own version of self-interest and economic survival above the societal responsibility of a free press.

Shirky suggests the mainstream media fail to understand that despite a participant's lack of skill or journalistic training, the Internet itself acts as an editing mechanism, with the difference that "editorial judgment is applied at the edges . . . after the fact, not in advance," as he wrote on the Networks, Economics and Culture mailing list in January.

Weblogs expand the media universe.

Seen in this light, Weblogs should not be considered in isolation but as part of an emerging new media ecosystem—a network of ideas. No one should expect a complete, unvarnished encapsulation of a story or idea at any one Weblog. In such a community, bloggers discuss, dissect and extend the stories created by mainstream media. These communities also produce participatory journalism, grassroots reporting, annotative reporting, commentary and fact-checking, which the mainstream media feed upon, developing them as a pool of tips, sources and story ideas. The relationship is symbiotic.

Lisa Rein, who videotaped the peace marches, borrows television news segments and retransmits them on her Weblog. She regularly records "Meet the Press" and presidential candidates' appearances on C-SPAN, then uploads the video clips to her blog, a practice she says is permitted under fair use. She also attends technology and law conferences, videotapes the speakers, and transfers that footage as well. The tools have become so easy to use that Rein—literally, a one-woman personal broadcast network—has attracted an international following. She now uploads video to her blog several times a day.

"There are just so many interesting things happening in our lives that would make great programming," she told me. "The networks aren't interested unless it will attract millions of dollars in advertising revenues. Meanwhile, there are people and events all around us that are meaningful and that people would love to watch."

Managing Editor Scott Rosenberg wrote in *Salon* [in 2002]: "Weblogs expand the media universe. They are a media life form that is native to the Web, and they add something new to our mix, something valuable, something that couldn't have existed before the Web.

"It should be obvious that Weblogs aren't competing with the work of the professional journalism establishment, but rather complementing it. If the pros are criticized as being cautious, impersonal, corporate and herd-like, the bloggers are the opposite in, well, *almost* every respect: They're reckless, confessional, funky—and herd-like."

Readers Become Part of the News Process

The emerging relationship between Weblogs and traditional journalism promises to be fitful and stormy. Earlier this year *The Washington Post*'s Leslie Walker suggested that readers will never be able to rely on Weblogs for dependable news and information because bloggers don't cling to the same "established principles of fairness, accuracy and truth" that traditional journalists do. Bill Thompson, a visiting lecturer in the journalism school at City University, London, wrote in Britain's *The Guardian*: "Blogging is not journalism. Period."

Perhaps. But there's another possibility: that journalists need to move away from the notion that journalism is a mysterious craft practiced by only a select priesthood—a black art inaccessible to the masses. We forget the derivation of the word journalist: someone who keeps an account of day-to-day events.

Years ago I met Frank McCulloch, a legendary editor at *The Sacramento Bee* and *Los Angeles Times* and an ex-Marine who was Saigon bureau chief for *Time* during the Vietnam War. An ink-stained member of the old guard, McCulloch believed that journalism was a simple thing. Find the right people. Ask the right questions. Write it up. "This ain't rocket science," he often said.

Exactly. Citizens are discovering how easy it can be to play reporter and publisher. To practice random acts of journalism, you don't need a big-league publication with a slick Web site behind you. All you need is a computer, an Internet connection, and an ability to perform some of the tricks of the trade: Report what you observe, analyze events in a meaningful way but, most of all, just be fair and tell the truth as you and your sources see it.

Bloggers can do that. Few bloggers fancy themselves journalists, but many acknowledge that their blogs take on some of the trappings of journalism: They take part in the editorial function of selecting newsworthy and interesting topics, they add analysis, insight and commentary, and occasionally they provide a first-person report about an event, a trend, a subject. Over time, bloggers build up a publishing track record, much as any news publication does when it starts out. Reputation filters—where bloggers gain the respect and confidence of readers based on their reputation for accuracy and relevance—and circles of trust in the blogosphere help weed out the charlatans and the credibility-impaired. If the blogs are trustworthy and have something valuable to contribute, people will return.

I'm constantly astounded at the breadth of knowledge displayed by bloggers on subjects as diverse as wireless networking, copyright infringement, sonnet poetry, and much more, all written with a degree of grace and sophistication. Many readers have begun to turn to gifted amateurs or impassioned experts with a deep understanding of niche subjects, rather than to journalists who are generalists and cover topics a mile wide but an inch deep.

Now, is all blogging journalism? Not by a long shot. Nor is it likely that blogging will supplant traditional media or, as some have suggested, that blogging will drive news organizations out of business. When a major news event unfolds, a vast majority of readers will turn to traditional media sources for their news fix. But the story doesn't stop there. On almost any major story, the Weblog community adds depth, analysis, alternative perspectives, foreign views, and occasionally first-person accounts that contravene reports in the mainstream press.

We need, then, to stop looking at this as a binary, either-or choice. We need to move beyond the increasingly stale debate of whether blogging is or isn't journalism and celebrate Weblogs' place in the media ecosystem. Instead of looking at blogging and traditional journalism as rivals for readers' eyeballs, we should recognize that we're entering an era in which they complement each other, intersect with each other, play off one another. The transparency of blogging has contributed to news organizations becoming a bit more accessible and interactive, although newsrooms still have a long, long way to go.

Old media may have something to offer the young turks of blogspace, too, in the trust department. Bloggers who dabble in the journalistic process would do well to study the ethics rules and conflict of interest policies of news organizations that have formulated a set of guidelines derived from decades of trial and error. The conventions of journalism—accuracy, credibility, trustworthiness and being straight up with your readers—are guideposts that any good blogger should engrave on her wall. More needs to be done to make this collaboration a deeper and more meaningful phenomenon.

Transparency of Reporting

"Journalists must invite their audience into the process by which they produce the news," Bill Kovach and Tom Rosenstiel write in their book "The Elements of Journalism." "This sort of approach is, in effect, the beginning of a new kind of connection between the journalist and the citizen. It is one in which individuals in the audience are given a chance to judge the principles by which the journalists do their work. The first step in that direction has to be developing a means of letting those who make up that market finally see how the sausage is made—how we do our work and what informs our decisions."

Many journalists who blog are doing just that—exposing the raw material of their stories-in-progress, asking readers for expert input, posting complete text of interviews alongside the published story, and writing follow-up stories based on outsiders' tips and suggestions. As for readers who blog, giving them a stake in the editorial process—by letting them provide meaningful feedback or suggesting story leads—increases loyalty and understanding and spurs them to share their positive experience with others.

The authors of a research study, "Interactive Features of Online Newspapers," sum it up this way: "Journalists today must choose. As gatekeepers they can transfer lots of information, or they can make users a smarter, more active and questioning audience for news events and issues."

Journalism is undergoing a quiet revolution, whether it knows it or not. Readers will always turn to traditional news sites as trusted, reliable sources of news and information—that won't change. But the walls are cracking. The readers want to be a part of the news process.

We will always need a corps of trained journalists to ferret out important stories, to report from remote locations, to provide balance and context to the news. But beside big media journalism we are starting to see a mixture of commentary and analysis from the grass roots as ordinary people find their voices and contribute to the media mix. Blogs won't replace traditional news media, but they will supplement them in important ways.

What's ahead? Certainly a much larger role for amateurs in the news process. Weblogs are only one part of the puzzle. For instance, in late June 2003, NHK (the Japan Broadcasting Corp.) carried news of a serious highway accident. The scene was carried live via video from a bystander who was playing the role of journalist by shooting the action with his portable camera phone. Mobloggers—tech-savvy users who post photos, video and text to Weblogs from their mobile devices—just held their first convention in Tokyo. In Daytona Beach, Florida, a janitor created his own one-man TV station and occasionally Webcasts live news events.

All of this portends important changes as journalism expands its tent to include citizen participation. Ultimately, bloggers and the phenomenon of grassroots journalism have just as meaningful a role in the future of news on the Net as do the professionals.

Benefits Blogging Brings to News Outlets

What benefits do Weblogs bring to journalism? Several.

Pushing the envelope. Weblogs are helping to expand the boundaries of experimental forms of transaction journalism. Freelance journalist Christopher Allbritton, a former reporter for The Associated Press, asked his Weblog readers to finance a trip to Iraq at the outbreak of hostilities there. Some 320 people donated more than $14,000 and helped him launch Back-to-Iraq.com. His readers then served as his editors during three weeks of dispatches during which Allbritton broke news on the fall of Tikrit and highlighted the Balkan-style ethnic tensions among Kurds, Arabs, Turkomen and Assyrians. Similarly, freelancer David Appell, a physics PhD who has written for *Nature*, asked his readers to donate $20 apiece to fund his investigation of the politics of the sugar industry. He wrote a report after raising $425.

Blogs could show that newspapers aren't monolithic corporations but a collaborative team of individuals with varying viewpoints. . . .

Influencing at the edges. We see sentiments first expressed on Weblogs bubble up into the mainstream media days or weeks after they first surface in the blogosphere. Similarly, all too often the mainstream media tend to dispose of stories in a fast-paced news cycle, with even important news events falling off their radar screen after 48 hours. Bloggers say, hold the phone, we're not done with this yet. Blogs keep stories alive by recirculating them and regurgitating them with new angles, insights and even newsworthy revelations. Weblogs were credited with helping to get the mainstream news media interested in the racially insensitive remarks by Senator Trent Lott that led to his resignation as Senate majority leader.

Enhancing reader trust. News organizations such as MSNBC, *The Providence Journal*, *The Dallas Morning News*, and *The Christian Science Monitor* have embraced the Weblog form in some part of their editorial operations. . . . These news organizations realize that Weblogs offer an opportunity for newsrooms to become more transparent, more accessible, and more answerable to their readers.

Independent journalists and pundits such as Andrew Sullivan, Doc Searls, and Joshua Marshall have found that publishing a Weblog increases their authority and credibility in the eyes of readers. *Time* magazine media critic James Poniewozik described the perception gap between the audience and the media about trust this way: "Journalists think trust equals accuracy. But it's about much more: passion, genuineness, integrity." Weblogs and a commitment to open dialogue instill trust in the relationship between news media and audience.

Repersonalizing journalism. Blogs present a vehicle for expressing thoughts and reportage that doesn't always fit the contours of a traditional news report. Television reviewers have begun blogging their experiences with network executives and Hollywood stars during the annual summer Television Critics Association press tour in Los Angeles. Political writers are using blogs to bring daily commentary to the campaign trail. But more important, blogs offer an opportunity for readers to hear a journalist's voice and personality. Newsroom-sanctioned Weblogs promise to show journalists as human beings with opinions, emotions and personal lives— and yes, with warts and foibles. Weblogs could usher in a refreshing new openness in newsrooms by attaching a face and personality to reporters. Blogs could show that newspapers aren't monolithic corporations but a collaborative team of individuals with varying viewpoints and who have more in common with their readers than they could possibly know from reading their print articles alone.

Fostering community. When journalism becomes a process, and not a static product, audiences discard their traditional role as passive consumers of news and become empowered partners with a shared stake in the end result. Weblogs offer one way to promote that kind of interactivity.

6

Blogging Is Not Journalism

Horst Prillinger

Horst Prillinger is a librarian and university lecturer in Vienna, Austria. He writes a blog, The Aardvark Speaks, *which he started in 2002.*

Blogs are not journalism because they do not fulfill its strict set of standards; even noted writers and journalists do not always maintain these standards in their own blogs. Blogs, however, are a revolutionary mass medium that is entirely separate from journalism. The idea of the "news" is evolving, and blogging allows people to create news that is personal and relevant to themselves. Most bloggers do not seek the objective truth or wish to write on "serious" or "important" topics; first and foremost, they want to express themselves and share their points of view.

A re you serious? In your weblog? And/or in the way you think (or talk) about weblogs? Do you think that there are way too many weblogs that don't really serve a purpose? Are you annoyed by cat pictures and 'cheese sandwich blogging'? Do you think there are too many weblogs that just are not serious enough?

I have to admit that I am not very serious in my weblog. For example, I have a guestblogger on my weblog every Sunday who happens to be a fluffy toy moose. His name is Haldur Gislufsson, and he is extremely popular among my readers, to the point that sometimes they are writing to ask if anything is wrong when he has not blogged anything in a while.

I intend to be very serious in this paper, though. In fact, I am so serious that some people, especially those who are very serious in their weblogs, may regard what I am about to say as blasphemy. I can take this risk easily because I do not take weblogging all that seriously. It is the phenomenon of weblogging itself that I take very seriously.

In this paper I will not distinguish between a 'weblog' and an 'online diary'. This is because what I am going to talk about is not so much a certain kind of content, but instead the medium through which all kinds of content are published—in the sense of 'regular, chronological online publication via weblog software for public perusal', even though the public perusal may not be fully intended as such.

Weblogs Are Not Journalism

And while I will be talking about a mass medium, I will not be talking about weblogs as journalism. In fact, there is this long-standing and sometimes rather intense debate whether weblogs will one day replace 'traditional' journalism, including the long-standing and sometimes rather intense debate whether weblogs are journalism or not.

This debate has gone on for quite a while, despite the fact that the answer is obvious: *of course weblogs are not journalism.* Weblogs can be used for journalism, but only a minuscule percentage are actually used for journalism. The large majority is something else. Weblogs are a medium, just like a newspaper or television is a medium. Whether something is journalism or not depends, however, not so much on the medium, as on the content.

My standard answer to people who insist on equalling the two is to say: *weblogging relates to journalism as using Microsoft Frontpage relates to web design.*

I am not a web designer just because I know how to use Frontpage. Knowledge of the tools does not automatically include knowledge of the rules. I need to know a lot that goes far beyond using a web page editor—essential things such as user interface design, information architecture, graphic design, usability, markup language, and more—to qualify as a web designer.

Similarly, I am not a journalist just because I am publishing a weblog. Publishing something on a daily basis is not journalism, it is *publishing*. That is not the same thing at all.

Journalism goes far beyond mere publishing in being very much about adhering to journalistic principles in your work, a work ethic if you wish. In this context, the Austrian media law uses the term *Sorgfaltspflicht* (duty of care), in other words, a journalist must by all means assure that s/he has done everything to assert that the published article is correct. This would include among other things:

- first-hand research

- use of multiple sources

- inclusion of different perspectives

- careful and conscientious verification of sources

- quality control through an editorial process before publication

- clear distinction between statement of fact and statement of opinion

I venture to say that from any sample of weblogs only a minuscule percentage fulfil even just one of these criteria. Note that I am not saying that there are not any weblogs that would count as journalism—there certainly are—, but what you typically get from weblogs is, mostly:

- republication of second- or third-hand news (thanks to RSS [Really Simple Syndication])

- multiple references to just one source

- the author's perspective only

- no verification of sources—weblogs as rumour mill

- instant publication—quality control, if any, is through reader feedback *after* publication

- a mixture of fact and personal opinion

Interestingly, some of the webloggers who are insisting most fervently on being regarded as journalists, are not really following these standards in their weblogs either. People like [writer] Andrew Sullivan may excel at commentary, opinion pieces and punditry, but again this is not journalism. Or take the following examples from [law professor and blogger] Glenn Reynolds' *InstaPundit.com*:

"PLENTY OF READER REVIEWS for Clinton's book over at Amazon now. You could write a dissertation in sociology or political science from these. And somebody probably will."

"STANDING UP for free speech."

"CNN's SOURCE is changing his/her story on Rumsfeld and interrogation notes [sic!] Ed Morrissey. This will get as much play as the original accusation?"

These are three full articles (repeat: three full articles) by someone who considers himself a journalist. I do not know what you would think if you found these in a newspaper, but you probably would not take Glenn Reynolds, who apparently has some 300,000 hits per day on his website, as seriously as people take him. Some of the sentences are not even proper English. The point here is, however, that his entries *do* make sense, but only in their function as a *link hub*. Remove the links from the text, and it becomes totally devoid of meaning.

The Mass Media Revolution

And here we see already the first way, or the first step in which weblogs are changing our perception of how news can be communicated: we are seeing that in addition to the direct communication via a written article, there is also the indirect communication via a mere hyperlink. Suddenly people who are creating *access points* to other people's articles seem to become as important as the people actually writing these articles.

But it does not end there.

We are in the midst of what we might call a mass media revolution, and it is exciting to see how weblogs are a part of this revolution. Which is why I wrote this paper in the first place—not to bash weblogs, but to point out why the fact that they are not journalism, but more of a *complement* to journalism, is the truly great thing about them, and why we must not limit ourselves to focussing on the 'serious' side of weblogs and instead also take a serious look at the non-serious side of weblogs. Weblogs are not journalism, *and that is the great thing about them.*

What is happening is that we are witnessing a fundamental change as to what we perceive as 'news'.

Making the Media More Democratic

As much as we are talking about democracy and equality, our society is still fundamentally hierarchic in that it differentiates between those who make the decisions for others, and those who are subject to these decisions. Even a democracy does not change that. You elect your politicians, they decide for you. Traditionally, and this has been changing slowly over the past decades, but traditionally, what is mostly communicated through the mass media and even more so, what ends up in history books, are almost exclusively the actions and decisions of this ruling class (the political elite) and what one could refer to as 'the extraordinary', singular events of enormous impact on, or of great entertainment value for a large number of people (always with a few exceptions of course).

In the 1970s and 1980s, there was a growing realization that the mass media were not truly democratic in that citizens were excluded from the journalistic process. In that period we have numerous examples of projects to make participation in the mass media possible for a larger number of people. That is the age of *Stadtteilfernsehen* in Germany, when experimental TV stations were set up for single city districts and everyone was invited to participate, and it is of course also mirrored in the increasing regionalisation of all kinds of mass media, but the traditional media never became truly 'democratic' in the meaning that *everyone* could participate, in that they lacked an infrastructure that was really open to a large number of participants.

This changed with the Internet. Contrary to previous forms of publishing, the Internet allowed more people than before to publish whatever they wished to publish. All you needed was Internet access, dedicated server space and an HTML editor. The Internet has an infrastructure that can (potentially) accommodate everyone, in terms of participation it is therefore (potentially) more democratic than any other mass medium.

Weblog software has taken this development one step further, because now all you need is Internet access, and you can publish your own 'news' every day if you wish, theoretically (depending on your weblog software) without any technical knowledge. This is a total transformation of the media landscape, a veritable mass media revolution: you now have the power to publish your 'news' on your own mass medium.

But what exactly is this 'news'?

The Metamorphosis of 'News'

In a development that has started already a few decades back, the definition of 'news' has started to change significantly in one particular direction, and it has gained more and more momentum as time progressed. We have been moving away from 'news that are relevant to the world' to 'news that are entertaining for the world', but more recently there has been a pronounced shift to 'news that are relevant to me'. In traditional media, this development has led to the proliferation of reality soaps, which are a misdirected and somewhat futile attempt to turn everyday life (and, of course, everyday voyeurism) into media content. What has happened, though, is that the way somebody brushes his teeth inside the *Big Brother* container is suddenly no less newsworthy than the latest events in Iraq.

And oddly, if you think about it, it even makes sense. In terms of direct relevance for a person's life, the events in a war thousands of miles away or the events in some weird container are first and foremost virtual. Knowledge of these things would not be there without the mass media in the first place, and both could be complete constructs, for the average consumer is perfectly unable to verify it personally without being in the location him- or herself. So, as harsh as this may sound, any emotional involvement is just as much a construct, depending on how much you trust or distrust the media, but not by what is actually happening somewhere.

Essentially, we live in a world of media constructs, in a world that is devoid of emotional involvement. Therefore, people are looking just for the kind of media content that provides this involvement, and, as there are now no longer locked out of the mass media, when they do not find it, they can use newly available publishing tools like weblog software to generate just this kind of content.

Which is why weblogs are often compared to, or even described as 'reality soaps'. Some of these weblogs are very aware of this:

"This blog [. . .] has been described by a friend as a mixture of [the television shows] 'The Osbournes', 'Absolutely Fabulous' and 'My Family.'"

Life, let's admit it, is often banal. Quite often, the news on TV are not the news that really affect me. I am most likely more affected by my daughter's new boyfriend, my cat's illness, or if my computer acts up than by the speech of some head of state in some foreign country. These are the things I am confronted with every day in the first place. News is what is new in *my* life, not really what is on TV. And up until the arrival of weblogs, that was exactly the kind of media content we did not have. And now we not only have it, but we can produce and publish it ourselves.

[W]eblogs generally do not fulfill the criteria of journalism, like research, duty of care, and all of that.

By the way, this kind of news has always existed. Only we called it 'gossip'. It has always had a tremendously important role in and impact on our lives. However, until very recently it never had a medium over which it could spread other than talking person-to-person.

In addition to this, in a world of constructs, of course nothing prevents people from publishing constructs themselves. You can also call it 'artistic expression'. If you feel you are not yet ready for publishing in book form, you can publish your writing on your website or weblog. In fact, you can publish anything you wish, which is why there is such a vast diversity of weblog content, including a lot of content that does not seem to make sense. Take for example, this bit from *The Dullest Blog in the World*, an oddly popular weblog:

> "A light in one of the rooms of my house was on. I decided that I didn't need the light on any longer. I pressed the light switch thereby turning off the light."

Weblogs Are Not About the Truth

Earlier on, I talked about how weblogs generally do not fulfill the criteria of journalism, like research, duty of care, and all that. That may have sounded like it was a bad thing. The point is, unless you take journalistic weblogs, or weblogs, as information sources, it does not matter. As a truly democratic medium, weblogs are not about truth. They are not about what is true or not, but about what concerns one particular person. Their whole point is one individual's distorted point of view. Their whole point is letting one individual express whatever is important to him or her.

[Bloggers] do not want to be journalists. They just want to be themselves.

And that is a great thing. If you think of it, the contents of people's weblogs give a considerably sharper picture of what really concerns people, of what they are dealing with in their everyday lives and of what these lives look like than any newspaper, TV show or other 'old media' format that I can think of.

A Mosaic of Everyday Life

In writing weblogs, people are generating little less than a mosaic picture of everyday life in the early 21st century, perhaps not of all people, but of a large enough social section. From a historical point of view, this kind of source material will give a picture that is radically different from what we find in our own history books.

Weblogs are not journalism, but hell, are they one revolutionary mass medium. And that is just because most webloggers do not take blogging all that seriously. They do not want to write just about what is considered 'serious', 'important' stuff by others, but only about what matters to themselves.

They do not want to be journalists. They just want to be themselves. They just want to express themselves. And that is why weblogs are so important: without weblogs, these people would not be able to express themselves and we would not learn who they are. And that possibility of public self-expression—including its consequences and even dangers, about which I am not going to talk about in this paper—is a very serious development.

Are you serious about expressing yourself?

7

Social Networking Connects People

Cade Metz

Cade Metz is PC Magazine'*s senior writer.*

The idea of social networks is not new, but advancing computer technology and the growing accessibility of broadband have helped social networking sites become a phenomenon. Though it may seem strange to create an Internet profile for all the world to see, millions of people log on to sites like MySpace and Tag-World everyday to keep in touch with friends and relatives, find long-lost classmates, and meet like-minded people. Also, the social networking rage is not just for young people; sites like Linke-dIn, LibraryThing, and The Mom Network have proven their appeal to older generations.

Unless you're completely out of touch with everyday American life, you know about the runaway popularity of MySpace. You've read the newspaper stories, heard the radio talk, and seen the skits on *Saturday Night Live*, so you know it's got to be hot.

The question is, should you care? Those of us old enough to have a 401(k) plan can't help but ask what the big deal is about MySpace and all of the other social-networking sites out there. Is this a cultural and technological phenomenon, or just a new way to goldbrick? Who uses them besides 19-year-old layabouts posting treatises on [reality TV show] *Laguna Beach* or pictures of Joey doing a keg stand at the Sigma Chi party last night?

Well, there's Daniel Boud, a 26-year-old Web designer and amateur photographer who posted his concert photos on Flickr, and they ended up in Rolling Stone. There's Joe Ford Jr., a 32-year-old lawyer from Tennessee, who is running for Congress mainly through a MySpace page. And 31-year-old schoolteacher Kathryn Smith, who lost nearly 30 pounds in a couple of weeks, thanks to the support she received on Peer-Trainer.

Okay, we'll also throw in Michael Block, a person of the "Joey doing a keg stand" ilk. A 24-year-old self-described ego-maniac from Manhattan Beach, California, Block posts photos of himself riding toy dinosaurs along the L.A. freeways. He reviews and rates every episode of *The O.C.* and proclaims his love for ranch dressing.

Mysteriously, people are interested. His TagWorld page receives more than 100 hits a day. Nearly 700 people have posted comments, and hundreds more show up on his "friends list," with their personal pages linked to his. Click on any one of the faces smiling back from his friends list, and you'll find a second friends list, linking to hundreds of other TagWorld fanatics. And on it goes into digital infinity.

Sweeping the Country

With 1.6 million personal pages, TagWorld is but a small part of the ever-growing phenomenon of social networking, which aims to link masses of like-minded people together. MySpace, the social-networking Goliath, receives nearly 12 million unique visitors a day, more than any domestic site save Yahoo!, Google, and MSN, according to the research firm comScore Media Metrix. Chances are that you've also heard about the big crowds visiting Flickr and YouTube, sites that bring the MySpace ethos to photo and video sharing.

The huge success of these media darlings has sparked what some are calling a second dot-com boom. In an ironic bit of deja vu, Internet startups are again proliferating like rabbits, each offering a site that puts a new spin on the notion of social networking. Not to be outdone, existing dot-coms are jumping on the bandwagon, adding social tools to their sites. And big names such as News Corp., the parent company of the FOX network, and Yahoo! are gobbling up these social startups, doing their best to stay ahead of the curve.

Geocities Revisited

Social networking isn't a new idea. In fact, it's the very idea that sparked the creation of the Web itself. When he dreamed up the World Wide Web, [Internet pioneer] Tim Berners-Lee envisioned a tool that would give a voice to the common man. The Internet would allow anyone to exchange information with anyone else around the world. As he wrote in his memoir, *Weaving the Web*, it would engender "the decentralized, organic growth of ideas, technology, and society."

Bringing people together is what all social-networking sites have in common. . . .

Unfortunately, as the Web rose to prominence in the mid-1990s, the hardware and software couldn't support this original vision. The average Joe didn't have enough bandwidth over dial-up to communicate easily with the Web at large. Without some serious computer know-how—or some serious cash—the best you could do was build a personal page on a clunky online service like GeoCities. GeoCities pages were woefully static and almost painfully unattractive—not to mention hard to find. They didn't really connect one person with another.

Thanks to broadband, sites like MySpace finally fulfill the Web's original promise. It's GeoCities on steroids—a better way of creating a personal Web page and serving it up to the world, complete with photos, video, music, and more. "The big difference is that broadband penetration has tripled in this country," says Randy Browning, who oversees social-networking research for the consulting arm of Pricewater-houseCoopers. "With GeoCities, it was nothing but blah content. Now you get the full multimedia experience." Flickr and, particularly, YouTube simply wouldn't be possible over dial-up.

How They Work

Bringing people together is what all social-networking sites have in common, but how and why they do this—some are just for fun; others are for achieving a goal such as finding a job—is where they differ.

Some sites, including TagWorld, operate along the lines of MySpace, predicated on the idea of letting you create a personal-profile page where you can share all sorts of random thoughts and multimedia content. Other users become your "friends," some of whom are complete strangers. From there, it's a popularity contest of sorts to see how many friends you can amass. So far, MySpace president Tom Anderson is the prom king, with more than 80 million friends.

Other sites, like Flickr and YouTube, are merely a repository of user-provided content. Buzznet, Flickr, and Zoto (among others) broadcast your digital photos. And eyespot, Grouper, and YouTube serve up your personal videos and hilarious, poignant, or bone-crushing moments captured from live TV. You can share your browser bookmarks on del.icio.us, your MP3s on Mercora, and the names of your favorite books on LibraryThing. The idea here is that you can get better results searching for specific content that's been hand-picked from the vast reaches of cyberspace. And most tagging sites will let you then follow the trail of breadcrumbs to see who posted the link you like and what other content he or she has to offer.

Sites like LinkedIn, which at three years old [in 2006] is one of social networking's pioneers, use existing business contacts as the roots for growing new ones. They're built on the notion of six degrees of separation—the idea that we're only six introductions away from anyone we'd want to meet. LinkedIn and similar six-degree sites such as Friendster, Ryze, Plaxo, and Tribe were the first to use the term social networking.

Some sites use the wildly popular concept of tagging as a tool to link people together. Users are encouraged to tag their information with keywords, a way of linking similar content. If you're an anime fan, for example, you can visit TagWorld, click on the "Anime" tag, and instantly browse all photos involving Japanese animation.

Once you've linked to the posts of other anime fans, you might find yourself browsing beyond their anime pics, into the rest of their photo collections, their music, their blogs. Who knows? You might develop a running online relationship—or even meet them in person.

We All Need To Be Loved

To the uninitiated, many of these sites may seem a bit odd. Why, you might ask, would you want the rest of the world to see you riding a plastic dinosaur? But, if you stop to think about it, it makes perfect sense—especially among the younger generation.

"This can all be summed up, whether we like it or not, with one word: attention," says Michael Block. "We're all starving for it, and all of these sites are just another way to get it." Granted, not everyone craves the kind of attention Block does. But he's right; people enjoy attention. And if you grew up on reality TV and celebrity tabloids, you might enjoy throwing yourself out there, warts and all, for the world to see, just as much as you enjoy consuming the lives of others who do the same.

"Our everyday culture definitely celebrates self-disclosure," says Susannah Stern, an assistant professor at the University of San Diego whose research focuses on adolescents and electronic media. "Kids are picking up on that. It gives them every indication that this is what we value from people."

[S]ocial networking isn't just for kids.

The danger is that this sort of self-disclosure can come back to haunt you. Prospective employers or university admissions officers may not like what they see on your MySpace page. And by now you've heard the stories about people trolling these sites with less than honorable intentions. There are ways, however, to control the content you post online.

What's important to remember when using social sites—the thing that many I'm-nothing-less-than-invincible teenagers may be slow to pick up on—is that certain information is best withheld from the public at large.

Clicks Aren't Just for Kids

Kathryn Shantz will be the first to tell you that social networking isn't just for kids. The 39-year-old has tried TagWorld and dabbled on MySpace, but LinkedIn keeps her coming back. Since joining the site in 2004, Shantz has built up rock-solid connections across the business world. Her LinkedIn profile—which amounts to an online resume—links to dozens of close friends and colleagues. They, in turn, link to their friends and colleagues. And if you're in sales, you can use the site to help potential clients find you online.

At one point, Shantz used the service to find a reliable freelance photographer for her Bay Area public relations firm. In recent months, she's used it to track down investors for a new startup called ArtSugar. "I look at other social sites as recreational, and I don't have a lot of time for them," she says. "LinkedIn has real value. I use it constantly."

John Bauer, a 37-year-old San Francisco resident, also discovered the power of LinkedIn. Bauer was working as a product manager at Wells Fargo when be noticed an interesting job posting and applied on a whim. He got the job and is now the worldwide director of Internet marketing at Logitech. "The quality of jobs posted on LinkedIn is a lot more refined than on other competing sites," Bauer says.

For those who do have time for recreational socializing online, sites like MySpace and TagWorld not only serve as a link to friends old and new, but they often become the perfect medium for ad hoc dating. And because they're free, they're often more attractive than online and real-world dating services. Even niche sites like LibraryThing sometimes play Cupid. LibraryThing's founder Tim Spaulding says his brother uses the bibliophile site to meet women.

The Mom Network (www.clubmom.com) is exactly what it advertises: an enormous network of mothers, spanning the globe. "My daughters call it MySpace for old people," says Sandra Hummel, an avid Mom Networker. But in the end, The Mom Network connects individuals who share common goals and interests, as well as swap very specific pieces of advice.

Hummel lives in El Paso, Texas, where her husband, a sergeant major in the army, is stationed at Fort Bliss. At press time, her family was weeks away from moving to Fort Irwin in California. Looking for the lowdown on Irwin, she used The Mom Network to find another military wife who was already stationed there. "In no time she sent me a list of all the local shopping malls," Hummel says.

Last year, Kathryn Smith, a 31-year-old middle-school teacher from Foster City, California, joined PeerTrainer, a social-networking site for weight loss. The site connects you with people who share your fitness goals, and as you swap daily eating and exercise habits with these peers, they provide the much-needed motivation and encouragement. It's like a Weight Watchers meeting you can attend at any time.

So Smith found a group of local women who, like her, wanted to lose 20 to 30 pounds. Within a few weeks, she'd lost the weight, and as a way of keeping it off, she continues to use the site every day. "You support each other. You congratulate each other," says Smith. "As the day goes on, you know you have to record everything you eat—and someone will be looking at it."

Countless other sites provide additional benefits. Much as LibraryThing provides book recommendations, Spout provides movie recommendations. AirTroductions, another site that encourages face-to-face meetings, provides a forum for people flying alone to find a simpatico flying companion.

Bringing the Family Online

Of course, many social sites are worth using simply because they connect you with friends and family. Even among the younger generation, this is the primary purpose of a site like MySpace. "Most of what they're doing is communicating with people they know, using the Web to maintain existing relationships," says Susannah Stern. "It's a really easy and convenient way for them to connect."

> [T]here's every indication that this generation will continue to use social networks as they get older. . . .

Ashley Imsand, a 21-year-old senior at Auburn University in Alabama, uses Facebook to trade notes and pictures with old high-school friends. "They're spread all across the country," she says. "It's a neat way to share what's going on in each other's lives. You manage to stay in touch more than you otherwise would."

Sandra Hummel's daughter, Darnelle, uses MySpace to communicate with friends back in Germany, where the family was stationed before moving to Fort Bliss. On several occasions, she's even used MySpace to track down friends and relatives that her family lost touch with over the years and after several moves. Other social sites, like Reunion.com and

Classmates, are designed for finding long-lost friends or relatives. You can perform a search and then contact that person through the site, without the other person seeing your contact info. And you can make sure those people stay in your life by adding them to your address book.

What the Future Holds

Today, the biggest sites appeal mainly to the younger generation. But, now that they're hooked, there's every indication that this generation will continue to use social networks as they get older—through they may use them in slightly different ways. Sites like LinkedIn already serve the older crowd, and more are on the way.

"I can't tell you if people will continue to use MySpace and Facebook," says Alan Winter, who tracks social networking for the Gartner research firm. "But I will tell you that they will continue to use many of the same sorts of tools that make these social communities so powerful."

Yes, there are problems to iron out. Some certainly involve privacy. And it remains to be seen how many of these sites can make money in the long run. No doubt, many will fade away. But others will make the grade on their own, and some, like Flickr and MySpace, will merge with much larger entities.

Winter comments, "It's analogous to what happened with e-commerce ten years ago. Every day, a new e-commerce company would pop up, and so many were great ideas. But, given the finite amount of time we humans have, not all of them could survive. That's likely what will happen with social sites. Many will fail, others will do really well, and some will be bought by a Google or a Microsoft or a Yahoo!, becoming part of a larger ecosystem. That's where we're headed."

It really is like a second boom—though startups are far more careful about finances. Everyone has at least some kind of business model. Like the first time around, there's a fair amount of unwarranted hype clouding the issue. But underneath it all, there's something that appeals to our most basic instincts.

If a site's getting 12 million hits a day, it must be on to something.

8

Social Networking Is Problematic

Molly Wood

Molly Wood is a section editor at CNET.com, *a technology-centered media Web site.*

Because of their lack of solid revenue, most social networking sites are in trouble and may go bust like the dotcoms did. Furthermore, there are five things wrong with social networking itself: social networking sites do not offer anything to do other than people-watch; they are too time-consuming to create and to maintain a profile on; the traffic of these sites will not guarantee revenue alone; meeting strangers on-line is overrated and circles become cliquish; and social networks are not as useful as Internet search tools for navigating through all the information in cyberspace.

The word on the street lately is that social networking is in trouble. Friendster's CEO, Scott Sassa (most famous for firing a blogger who wrote about the company) recently departed in the face of a rapidly dwindling user base. Friendster has also introduced its own for-pay blogging tool as an all-too-ironic money-making scheme. Business networking site LinkedIn started charging for its job listings. Meanwhile, the recent launch of the Yahoo 360 beta has the blogosphere speculating that Friendster, the pioneer, is already on its deathbed. And [magazine] Business 2.0 has a good article . . . about how the indie music networking site MySpace is, for all intents and purposes, the only-successful site, with more than $20 million in ad sales this year and plenty of long-staying subscribers.

Social networking is laboring under the inescapable weight of the dot-com curse: you have to find the money. No matter how cool your idea is, it's dead on arrival without an actual business plan. At least, that's the theory. If that's true, though, why has blogging, which seems like a neat idea dependent on interest but without a concrete revenue stream, managed to not just thrive, but really dominate the Web? How is it that free instant messengers are as indispensable as any search engine, and little guys like [instant messaging application] Trillian are still going strong? Is it really true that free services can't be effective business plans? Or is it possible that—gasp!—social networking isn't really that tenable an idea after all?

The Social Networking Experience

I've gotten a lot of invitations to Friendster over the years, which, to be honest, I ignored. I always just assumed I didn't have time for that tomfoolery. Plus, I already had a boyfriend, and I already had friends. I know that all sounds horribly snobby, but there it is. But then, along came Orkut. Suddenly, because I was working in the Geek Zone, my coworkers were sending me Orkut invites. Every geek I knew was into it, and the peer pressure got too strong. I signed up. I filled out my little Orkut profile (I think I even uploaded a photo), and for about three weeks, my friends, coworkers, and I obsessively hung out on Orkut. And then, suddenly, we just got bored—weirdly, all at the same time. My entire Orkut generation, all the people who'd found it at the same time I did, just up and lost interest. Of course, round about that time, Orkut got painfully slow, and although it's better now (I just checked it out in the course of writing this column—hey, maybe I'll have a resurgance of interest!), it's still a heck of a lot easier to just e-mail or instant-message the people I know.

The Five Horsemen

Therein, I think, lies one of the five problems I've identified with social networking, and a good segue into my list.

1. There's nothing to do there As Business 2.0 points out, a simple destination site won't cut it. My big beef with Friendster was always, "Well, what would I *do* there?" Visiting most social networking sites is akin to getting invited to a party where all the cool kids are going, then showing up and finding out there's no food, no drinks, no band, no games, no pool, nothing. Just a bunch of painful small talk and leering grins. The people-watching can hold your interest for only so long.

2. It takes too much time Yes, I know I can choose where to devote my time, but Orkut, Friendster, and even LinkedIn (which I do find more useful than the purely social sites) are interesting but less information rich than news sites, blogs, Google news, or any of the other sites I could visit on the Web. It's interesting, for example, to blog about the experiences I had on a given day, but its tedious to make sure my personal stats, favorite books, and current reading list are up-to-date. One of the reasons I think personal blogs win out over social networking is that they're inherently more personal, more inwardly focused, and a better chance to show more than a snapshot of yourself.

3. Traffic alone isn't enough The reality of the new Web is that traffic alone just doesn't cut it. You can get all the visitors you want to your site, but you can't just blanket the thing with ads and hope to survive. Advertisers today are a more sophisticated bunch, and they're looking to send targeted, rich-content messages. That means that reliance on a generalized supply of banner ads is not a sustainable model, because no matter how much data you collect about your audience, if the audience isn't specific, the ads can't be, either. Witness MySpace's projected $20 million in ad sales. According to Business 2.0, it's working because MySpace attracts primarily what it refers to as "16- to 34-year-old hipsters." The Web is becoming an elitist sort of space. If social networking sites are a way to bring the masses together, advertisers are begging for a way to prune those masses into smaller, easier targets.

4. Strangers kind of suck (or, put nicely, the social hierarchy is really not that attractive) Speaking of elitism, getting to know people is, frankly, a less attractive proposal than it first seems. Sure, business networking is valuable, and it's great to have a lot of resources who might know someone who can help you with . . . something. But that argument gets a little thin when you're suddenly bombarded with date offers or all-too-frequent postings about the unsavory or just plain uninteresting habits of the strangers you suddenly know. Moreover, social networking sites pretty quickly and inevitably degenerate into cliques. That's normal, it happens on the blogosphere, and it's not really even that deplorable. It's just kind of tiresome on a daily basis. If you restrict your friends list to only the people you already know, well, then the boredom sets in. Why would you read their profiles over and over when you can just IM [instant message] them, e-mail them, or meet at the baseball game?

5. We already have the Internet The only lasting argument about social networking that's ever made sense is that these networks are a valuable resource if you're adrift in the sea of online information. You can, in just a few hops, get to someone who knows someone or knows something that you need to know. That *may* be a valuable proposal in the business world, which gives a site like LinkedIn a better chance of survival than Friendster. But the argument's a little thin in a world where search is the king of the hill. If I need information online, I can find it. And I can probably find it faster using Google than I can by e-mailing one friend who'll e-mail another who'll e-mail another while my deadline slips away. Sure, it's helpful—once in a while. But once I have all these folks in my address book, I won't be much help in terms of ad impressions.

9

Viral Videos Will Revolutionize Entertainment

Adrian McCoy

Adrian McCoy is a staff writer for the Pittsburgh Post-Gazette.

Viral videos, the creating, sharing, and viewing of homemade and amateur video clips online, is exploding in popularity and will change the face of entertainment. Jaded by mass-marketed Hollywood films and overly produced prime-time television series, viewers across the globe download 100 million viral videos a day, which will have a lasting impact on the marketing and distribution of mainstream movies and television shows. Also, as more ordinary people create their own viral videos, a whole new set of stars will emerge—without the help of major studios and networks.

Andy Warhol [American pop artist] famously observed that in the future, everyone would be famous for 15 minutes. That day is here, although the average minute count stands between two to five. Andy, who once made a 24-hour film of the Empire State Building and whose own improv-driven films featured unknowns and wannabes, would have loved the video-sharing phenomenon.

In the past year, the online universe of user-created videos has exploded and is expanding at an ever-increasing rate. Sites like YouTube—whose slogan is "Broadcast Yourself"—and a host of others give anyone, anywhere, the chance to star in their own reality show, with a potential global audience.

For those of us who are easily amused and have a high-speed Internet connection, it's possible to drift online for hours, watching video clips of just about anything you can imagine—would-be musicians and athletes strutting their stuff, people sharing their innermost thoughts and feelings, stupid pet tricks and even weirder human performances. . . . The only limit is the human imagination.

YouTube, one of the leading video sharing sites, made headlines [in October 2006] when search engine giant Google purchased the company for $1.65 billion. The deal shows how seriously mainstream media companies are taking an Internet phenomenon that's only a few years old—and has yet to show a profit. YouTube users tune in an estimated 100 million videos a day. The majority of the audience is in the teens and 20s.

Many of the big online forces like Google, Yahoo, AOL and MSN have their own versions of YouTube. MSN's new Soapbox—an invitation-only service—is scheduled to expand in the coming weeks. And there are a host of independent sites, many of which are exploring new technologies and ways to make it easier for more people to upload their videos.

Breaking Down Barriers

There appears to be an undeniable appeal to a rough five-minute video over a network TV program that's passed through all the layers of focus groups and network suits.

"User-generated content breaks down the falsified barriers between audience and creator," says Justin Kownacki, a Pittsburgh-based artist and creator of the Web series "Something to Be Desired." "Folks who enjoy sharing video and audio online are drawn to the imperfections, the work-in-progress feel. It allows a viewer to feel much closer to the process and the creators than a slick Hollywood film or prime-time television show can ever hope to achieve, because their very methods create a distance between themselves and the audience."

Kownacki's Web-based soap opera, now in its fourth season, revolves around a young group of friends living and working in Pittsburgh and features many recognizable locations as a backdrop. Kownacki has used several video-sharing sites in the past for his video shows, including YouTube and Motionbox, and now works with blip.tv.

Video-sharing is a revolution fueled by the viral video phenomenon—online video clips that become popular by Internet word of mouth: e-mails, blogs and instant messaging.

Anyone with a video camera and Web savvy can record and upload short videos. Many mobile phones and digital cameras have video recording capabilities as well, making it even easier for more people to create videos.

To watch them, one needs a high-speed Internet connection—or dial-up and a ton of patience. Most sites use Adobe Flash Player to show selected clips. Others use QuickTime or Windows Media Player.

The cinematography varies just as widely as the subject matter: from well-paced, well-edited clips, some by aspiring professionals, to jerky footage straight out of "The Blair Witch Project."

There are three kinds of video sharing going on:

One is on the personal level: friends and families exchanging video milestones online, e.g. little Jimmy's first steps or the trip to Disney World.

The second kind is more public, with people posting videos for the entire planet to watch. Some attract thousands of viewings, others much less. Parents take note: Because of some of the content's unedited and uncensored nature, supervision for young viewers is strongly recommended.

The third group of online content creators is more professional, and the first wave in a massive sea change in the entertainment industry.

New York-based blip.tv is an example of the latter, serving as a platform and distributor for original Web-based shows.

"We have people who are essentially creating original and serialized TV shows," says blip.tv co-founder and chief operating officer Dina Kaplan. The site features short programs, around five minutes long, in several genres, including citizen journalism, music, comedy, environmental issues, science and video blogging.

We're in the midst of a massive video revolution.

Kaplan, who grew up in Squirrel Hill [a Pittsburgh neighborhood], sees online video as a new outlet for creative talent.

"Instead of dreaming about a show, you can create a show. The best content will rise to the top, and the possibilities are endless for anybody who wants to create a show or star in one."

The Ultimate Democratization

In the era of reality TV and American idols, it's becoming a new way for aspiring talent to get seen. Cleveland hip-hop artist Denny Blaze's "Average Homeboy" video made it to VH1 and also is popular on both YouTube and Google sites. The phenomenon already has generated stars such as Lonelygirl, a teen expounding on her world from her room, and Little Loca, a Latino girl with lots of attitude—both are fictional characters played by actresses.

Web programmers are excited about the future of this relative new medium, and its impact on film and TV.

Says Kownacki, "The '70s was the age of film-school graduates—[Steven] Spielberg, [George] Lucas, [Martin] Scorsese—taking over Hollywood, and the '90s saw music-video directors—David Fincher, Spike Jonze, McG—make the leap. The 2000s are the era of a new breed of amateur filmmaker who will soon be leading the charge to change the way mainstream films are created, structured, marketed and distributed.

"YouTube is the first popularized service for these film-makers, but it certainly won't be the last."

"We're in the midst of a massive video revolution," Kaplan adds. "What we consider a TV show will be enormously different five years from now.

For years, network executives have made the programming decisions, she says. "Now the people can decide. It's the ultimate democratization."

10

Many Viral Videos Infringe Copyright Laws

Scott D. Marrs and John W. Lynd

Scott D. Marrs and John W. Lynd are partners at the law firm Beirne, Maynard & Parsons in Houston, Texas, representing clients in intellectual property litigation.

Many viral videos posted and shared on sites like YouTube contain copyrighted footage and amount to infringement. The owners of copyrighted footage do not benefit from viral videos because the content is not viewed as it was intended and is distributed without charge. In addition, instances in which copyrighted footage is appropriated, especially to create video "mashups," represents the unique and complicated problem of "fair use" of the content. Though taking action against every single instance of infringement and revenue loss through viral videos may be impossible, copyright owners can partner with video sharing sites to stop or manage unauthorized use or sharing and swiftly pursue the remedies made available by copyright laws.

What is "viral video?"

When a video clip spreads quickly across the Web, it is described as "going viral." You have likely already encountered viral video, those sometimes interesting, amusing or even entertaining pieces of video attached to e-mail messages like: "Check this out, it's hilarious!" But where did that video footage come from, who owns it and what are the economic and legal implications of this activity?

These video clips usually originate on viral video Web sites (free video-sharing sites), where users of the site can view, upload, download and share clips with others, spreading the clip far and wide, literally worldwide, without cost, and often without the permission of the owner of the copyrighted video footage.

Viral video is proliferating on the Web in two ways: first, through the straightforward posting and sharing of video clips without modification, and, second, through the visual remixing of copies of clips. The remixed video is often referred to as a "mash-up," where different video materials are juxtaposed together, or where numerous clips from one film or television show are borrowed and compiled with altered dialogue or theme music, for comic effect. These mash-ups are then posted on viral video sites and shared.

What does viral video mean to television networks, movie studios and other owners of copyrighted video material? The viral use of copyrighted material without the owner's permission ultimately has a detrimental effect, since the work is not being viewed by the public in its intended form or location. The copyright owner derives economic benefit when the video is viewed in its intended location, namely, in movie theaters, via rented or purchased DVD/video recordings, on its television channel or on its own Web site (or a site licensed to stream that content). After all, that is why "works of authorship" are given protection under the law. Viral video represents the use without charge of another's intellectual property.

Copyright owners are beginning to realize the full import of what was once only a pesky problem. NBC Universal Inc. recently [as of 2006] led an investigation of free video-sharing sites where its copyrighted material was being used without license. The site, YouTube.com, was acting as a conduit for the free sharing of a 2 1/2-minute spoof rap (entitled "Lazy Sunday: Chronicles of Narnia") from NBC's *Saturday Night Live*. NBC served YouTube with a "cease and desist" notice demanding it remove this footage and approximately 500 other clips from its site or face legal proceedings for copyright infringement. YouTube immediately complied.

It has been reported that NBC then engaged in a "search-and-destroy" mission to shut down other free video-sharing sites where its copyrighted material was being used without permission. Although it has refused to identify the sites it has investigated, NBC has indicated that it uncovered more than 3,000 videos being shared without permission, including entire episodes of its television show *Will and Grace*, the feature-length movie *Brokeback Mountain* and hours of NBC's coverage of the recent Winter Olympics.

Copyright Issues

Is viral video copyright infringement, and if so, what remedies are available to copyright owners? This article assumes that the video clips being used by video sharing sites are protected by the Copyright Act. Although Congress established a voluntary system of registration, it created incentives for copyright owners to register their copyrights. The most significant benefit to registering copyrights under the act is the right to enforce a copyright in federal court. Infringement suits are the mechanism through which other important incentives and remedies created by the act operate.

For example, when actual damages are difficult to ascertain or a creative work has seemingly little extrinsic value, statutory damages are available. Statutory damages can be between $750 and $30,000 for each infringing work. Damages can therefore add up quickly when, as with viral video, there are sites sharing thousands of clips of copyrighted material without the owners' permission. If the court finds that the infringement was willful, it may increase the award of statutory damages to $150,000 per infringed work. Equally important in the litigation context, a certificate of registration is prima facie [on first appearance] evidence of copyright validity. For copyright owners hesitant to engage in the long and expensive process of litigation, costs and attorney fees for prevailing parties may be recovered. Finally, and perhaps most important, a registrant can obtain an injunction against an infringer.

[T]he courts are likely to conclude that the posting of video clips . . . and their subsequent sharing represents copyright infringement. . . .

NBC succeeded in stopping the activities of YouTube without resorting to litigation. However, if an owner of copyrighted video material does file suit against an alleged infringer for viral video activities, it will have to convince a court that this kind of video sharing constitutes copyright infringement. There are two things a plaintiff must prove to establish a prima facie case of copyright infringement: that it owns the allegedly infringed material (i.e., it is the copyright owner), and that the alleged infringer violated at least one of the exclusive rights granted to the plaintiff. Those rights include the exclusive right to reproduce the copyrighted work, to prepare derivative works based upon the copyrighted work, to distribute copies of the work and to display the work publicly.

The U.S. Supreme Court held recently in *MGM Studios Inc. v. Grokster Ltd.* (2005), that a distributed file-sharing system commits copyright infringement when its principal object is the dissemination of copyrighted material. The foundation of this holding was a belief that people who post or download music files without the copyright owners' permission are primary infringers. This activity is directly analogous to the activities of viral video sites. Therefore, the courts are likely to conclude that the posting of video clips to these sites and their subsequent sharing represents copyright infringement, and are activities for which the remedies mentioned above are available. A caveat to this conclusion, however, is that although the posting and sharing of unaltered video clips without the copyright holder's permission represents infringement, matters are not so clear-cut with regard to video remixes or mash-ups.

Mash-ups and Fair Use

A recent example of a video remix/mash-up is a clip entitled "Must Love Jaws." This remix includes excerpts from the 1975 classic movie *Jaws*, and is recast as a feel-good *Free Willy*-type aquatic adventure for comic effect. This example illustrates the fact that video remixes or mash-ups are derived from the pre-existing work or works used to make the remix or mash-up. A derivative work is defined as a work based upon one or more pre-existing works and that includes works that recast, transform or adapt that pre-existing work to create something new. Video remixes fall within this category. The right to prepare derivative works belongs exclusively to the copyright owner. Therefore, the use of video clips in this way, without the copyright owner's permission, is arguably, on its face, also copyright infringement.

If charged with copyright infringement, mash-up artists will likely assert the statutory defense of fair use. When confronted with this defense, the Copyright Act provides that a court must take into account the purpose and character of the use, including whether it is of a commercial nature or is for nonprofit educational purposes; the nature of the copyrighted work; the amount and substantiality of the portion used in relation to the copyrighted work as a whole; and the effect of the use upon the potential market for, or value of, the copyrighted work. These factors and their application to any fair use determination depend heavily upon the individual facts and circumstances of each case.

In *Campbell v. Acuff-Rose Music Inc.* (1994), the Supreme Court held that commercial parody may be considered "fair use." The court held that the 6th U.S. Circuit Court of Appeals did not give sufficient consideration to the nature of the parody involved in that case (2 Live Crew's rap parody of Roy Orbison's song "Oh, Pretty Woman") and had placed too much weight on the song's commercial character and the amount of content borrowed from the original. The court carried out an exhaustive analysis of the fair-use factors in reaching its decision to reverse the 6th Circuit's ruling.

Although concurring, Justice Anthony Kennedy had some words of warning to those who would interpret the court's ruling as blanket permission for parodists to infringe the copyrights of others: "[P]arody may qualify as fair use only if it draws upon the original [work] to make humorous or ironic commentary about that same composition. . . . As future courts apply our fair use analysis, they must take care to ensure that not just any commercial take-off is rationalized post hoc as a parody."

In light of the holding in *Campbell*, some analysts have assumed that video remixes/mash-ups currently proliferating on the Web (such as "Must Love Jaws") are now free game and shielded from assertions of copyright infringement by the fair use defense. However, this is not a certainty, and much will depend on the nature of the activity involved, and whether the remixers want to run the risk of being hauled into federal court to face allegations of copyright infringement and then have to rely upon the fair use defense, which will always be subject to the discretion of the fact finder, and thus prone to uncertainty.

Tips for Copyright Owners

If faced with infringing activities, copyright owners should be aware that a cause of action for infringement accrues when one has knowledge of a violation or is chargeable with such knowledge. In a case of continuing infringement, however, an action may be brought for all acts that accrued within the three years preceding the filing of the suit.

> *Viral video may amount to free publicity, but it ultimately results in no immediate or tangible economic benefit to the copyright owner. . . .*

Copyright owners should also be aware that their rights to pursue injunctive relief and/or a claim for actual or statutory damages may be barred by the doctrine of copyright estoppel. This doctrine applies when the alleged infringer can show that the copyright owner knew the facts of the infringement; the copyright owner intended its conduct to be acted upon or acted in a manner giving the alleged infringer a right to believe it was so intended (in other words, the copyright owner led the alleged infringer to believe that it didn't mind the infringing activity); the alleged infringer is ignorant of the true facts; and the alleged infringer relies on the copyright owner's conduct to his detriment.

Further, a copyright owner can be estopped not only by words and actions, but also by silence and inaction. The message to copyright owners is: Act as soon as these types of activity come to light, and utilize the remedies available under the Copyright Act if matters cannot be resolved by other means. Of course, viral video by its nature proliferates and propagates easily, and takes on a life of its own, making it a daunting task for anyone, even the largest network or studio, to investigate and take action against every instance of infringement.

How may copyright owners address viral video without pursuing infringement action? Viral video may amount to free publicity, but it ultimately results in no immediate or tangible economic benefit to the copyright owner, which is, after all, the primary benefit to copyright protection. However, it is apparent from the number of people viewing and sharing video clips and video remixes that there is a demand. It has been reported that NBC's investigation revealed that some of its videos had been downloaded more than 5 million times. The question then is, given the popularity of viral video, despite its legal implications and the remedies available to copyright owners under the law, should television networks and movie studios take a different approach (other than litigation) to this phenomenon?

Infringement Demands Pragmatic Solutions

One suggested solution is for television networks and other video copyright owners to partner with the most popular sites. It has been reported that a few established media companies have formed partnerships with YouTube:

> "Independent recording label Matador Records is [promoting] the band Pretty Girls Make Graves by allowing viewers to submit music videos for its upcoming single. Cable network MTV2 has provided clips from upcoming programming including 'The Andy Milonakis Show' that links back to the MTV2 Web site. Even advertisers are on board, as Nike has seeded the site with video clips promoting its footwear. This week, Disney's Dimension Films entrusted YouTube with the trailer for its upcoming film 'Scary Movie 4,' which promptly garnered 200,000 streams in its first 15 hours on the site."—Andrew Wallenstein, "Viral video site poses challenge for Hollywood-As YouTube takes off, media companies try to decide if it's friend or foe," *Hollywood Reporter*, March 21, 2006.

Another proposed solution is the establishment of an organization modeled on the existing performing rights societies which include the American Society of Composers, Authors and Publishers, Broadcast Music Inc. and the Society of European Stage Authors and Composers. Thousands, perhaps even millions, of times each day, musical works are performed publicly on the radio and on the Internet. Every performance represents a possible source of revenue for the copyright owner. However, given the huge numbers of broadcasts involved, this presents an insurmountable management problem for individual copyright owners.

In order to address this problem, composers and publishers of musical works have formed performing rights societies to control access to their works, license and police their use, and distribute fees/royalties collected to participating members by pooling their rights. Video copyright owners may consider forming an analogous organization to control the use of video footage (television shows, movies, etc.). This could provide an economical and centralized process for the legal use of copyrighted video footage with consistent results and appropriate remuneration to copyright owners.

In conclusion, viral video often constitutes copyright infringement, and remedies are available to copyright owners to address that activity. Although the posting and sharing of video clips is without doubt free publicity, it is also the free use of the owner's intellectual property, resulting in a loss of revenue to the owner. The very nature of this activity, its proliferation and the all but impossible task of policing every instance of infringement demands pragmatic solutions to its future management.

11

Podcasting Is a Powerful Medium

Dave Slusher

Dave Slusher is a software engineer based in Chicago, Illinois. He blogs and podcasts on his Web site, The Evil Genius Chronicles.

Podcasts are digital media files that are shared online and can be played back on computers and MP3 players. Many follow a "radio show" format, and audiences can subscribe to podcasts through Web feeds. Though still a new medium, podcasting has untapped potential because producing and distributing podcasts is simple and low cost. Nearly anyone with a computer and a microphone can podcast a show on any topic and genre imaginable. Podcasting also offers independent musicians, bands, and record labels the opportunity to directly reach their niche audiences. It is only a matter of time before podcasts become a hugely popular entertainment option.

The future of podcasting is a tough nut to crack, considering that there is so little present and past to it. I was in this pyramid scheme early—listening to podcasts, creating them, and writing tools to handle them. Even now [in February 2005], those days are less than 6 months old. This mode of communication and distribution is powerful and caught the public imagination in a big way. I've never seen something take off so quickly, especially not a whole new communication infrastructure. Of course, being built out of barely repurposed bits of existing infrastructure helped out a lot with that.

Dave Slusher, "The Future of Podcasting," www.ktoddstorch.com, February 11, 2005. Reproduced by permission.

Let me divide this look ahead into a few sections—what I want to happen, what I fear will happen, and what I expect to happen.

What I Want from the Future of Podcasting

It's hard to define exactly what I want podcasting to bring, because what I most want is to have a landscape created that I can't recognize. Podcast has a low cost of entry, low cost of production and reasonably low cost of distribution (this is what ends up hurting people who become unexpectedly popular, that shocking moment when the first bandwidth bill shows up). I want all of that to fuel a rewriting of the rules, an unleashing of imagination that will lead to new formats, new types of listening that seem obvious in retrospect that none of us were bright enough to create. I'd have never dreamed that there would be popular podcasts about bowel movements and jostling testicles, but there are.

I want to see new and different forms of drama come about. I'd love to see an independent film promote itself not just like Skinnybones—a podcast about the production—but with drama set in and around the film. It would be wildly interesting to listen to a podcast that gives the backstory as an audio play. Novelists could do similar and create scripts from the excised scenes and thus create audio plays that don't merely adapt another work but expand and fill in the gaps and create a deeper involvement with the story and characters.

I want the creators down the long tail to use this medium as their mechanism for getting into the attention economy. Indie bands and record labels need to realize this is a huge opportunity for getting their music out into the ears of potential listeners. Michael Butler and his band American Heartbreak are already doing this. I've heard dozens if not hundreds of great bands that are too good to be so deeply underappreciated. Podcasting offers them an opportunity to get out there, to do a better job at lowering the friction in matching the right music with the right listener. They are out there, and with less work than ever, creators can enable their potential fans to find them.

Most of all, what I want from podcasting is to instill in a whole new generation of people a love of the audible. Seventy years ago, the audio was a primary mode of interaction as family gathered around the radio for FDR [Franklin D. Roosevelt] Fireside Chats or [comedy duo George] Burns and [Gracie] Allen. Part of what drives my affection of podcasting is displaced affection for radio—affection that the bland commercial and public offerings of the present day have forfeited. I want to hear people taking chances and trying new things. It's been decades since I heard that on the corporate commercial airwaves, and it has been a rarity even on the public bands. Give me back my ears, allow me to enjoy listening to entertainment again. Is that so much to ask?

What I Fear from the Future of Podcasting

Much of what I like about the podcasting game is that has such a low ante. Nothing prevents big players, in the form of existing stations or show producers, from publishing. On the other hand, nothing prevents any individual with access to a computer, a network connection and a cheap microphone from creating one either. My fear is that the existing media oligarchs will not just enter this arena, but try to establish artificial gates to preclude individuals from podcasting.

The beauty of podcasting is that it can allow for creativity to run amok.

I think it would be great to have the largest radio shows distributed via podcast. If I could get the Howard Stern show that way, I would listen. I fear that rather than the media oligarchs embracing this world and allowing it to exist as a level playing field, one of two options might happen. The first is that they ignore it completely. The second is that [media companies] Viacom or Clear Channel or Infinity work to lobby for regulation or some form of rules that favor the large organizations, much like they and the RIAA [Recording Industry Association of America] did for the webcasting rules with the Library of Congress.

The beauty of podcasting is that it can allow for creativity to run amok. The oligarchs are in the business of putting out the same old same old (they don't have to be, but that's what they've chosen to make of it) and as such are the natural enemies of creativity, of the long tail. My hope is that long tail thinking prevails, my fear is that the enormous resources in the tall head will attempt to un-level the playing field to give the large organizations an unnatural advantage.

What I Expect from the Future of Podcasting

The future is arriving at an alarming rate. To make a guess about what the near and far future will hold is difficult. I firmly expect that there will be quite a bit of turnover in the roster of most popular podcasts. Much has been made of the power law and the effect of the top podcasts referencing each other to the exclusion of others. In practice, I think we will see more new popular podcasts and a number of current highly listened ones dropping in relative popularity. I don't think this will necessarily come from a decrease in listeners but in a lagging behind of gaining new ones. I think the market for podcasts will expand several orders of magnitude in the coming months and years.

I predict in a few years it will be transparent and not something with so much "buzz". When a listener looks to be amused or entertained, they will have a range of choices that include television, DVDs, radio, podcasts, webcasts. Podcasting will simply take a place as one more distribution method in a continuum of methods. It will become commercially exploited, people will make money off it, and I predict that much of this money will come in ways no one is expecting or predicting (i.e., not advertising or the standard models from previous media). Not only do I expect that, I am on the edge of my seat waiting for it.

The coming times will be interesting, possibly in the Chinese curse sense. Many people will find their horizons broadened, their connections widened and the distance of this planet shrink as our reaches expand. Engaging with and learning about other cultures will get easier and easier. Finding entertainment options will require ever less time and energy. The TiVo on-demand model will move from the TV to the ears, the listeners will be more empowered and will not have to listen to something that doesn't meet their needs because "it is the best thing on."

I can't wait.

12

User-Generated Content Threatens Advertising

Andrew Keen

Andrew Keen is a technology entrepreneur and the author of The Cult of the Amateur: How the Democratization of the Digital World Is Assaulting Our Economy, Our Culture, and Our Values. *He lives in Berkeley, California.*

Commercial spots created by consumers, or user-generated advertisements, are making big waves but to the serious detriment of the advertising industry. User-generated advertising amounts to a talent show for novices and pales in comparison to the artfully produced commercials of seasoned television and film veterans. The low cost of amateur videos, however, poses a bigger threat; every time a company chooses user-generated advertisements over professionally created commercials to save on advertising dollars, talented screenwriters, camera operators, audio engineers, and other professionals lose their foothold in the economy.

It's amateur hour at the Super Bowl this year [2007]. On Sunday [February 4], 90 million television viewers on CBS will be subjected to commercials made by "You"—*Time* magazine's Person of The Year for 2006. Three Super Bowl XLI advertisers—Doritos, the National Football League, and Chevrolet—will be running 30 second commercial spots made by amateurs. The Web 2.0 revolution in user-generated content has infiltrated the American living room. These amateur creators, who *Time* praise as "people formerly known as consumers," are now providing the entertainment at the biggest event in the media calendar.

This is not good news. The shift from professionally produced to user-generated advertising makes us poorer in both economic and cultural terms. The arrival of user-created commercials at Super Bowl XLI represents the American Idolization of traditional entertainment—degeneration of professional content into a "talent show" for amateurs.

We, the conventional television audience, are certainly losers in this new fashion for user-generated advertisements. We have traditionally watched Super Bowl commercials to be entertained by memorable ads. Often, these commercials are more memorable than the game. Occasionally, they even represent significant cultural moments in American history. Few of us, for example, can remember who won Super Bowl in 1984 (Los Angeles Raiders 38, Washington Redskins 9), where it was played (Tampa), or who sang the national anthem (Barry Manilow). But most of us can remember the [advertising agency] Chiat/Day produced, [English film director] Ridley Scott directed, commercial for the Macintosh computer, with its Orwellian subtext and its indelible explanation of why "1984 wasn't going to be like 1984".

Don't expect a repeat of Chiat/Day and Ridley Scott's creative genius, during Super Bowl XLI. Doritos are already previewing the five finalists in their competition on the Yahoo! website. One commercial features a chip-chomping rock climber falling off a mountain; another has a giant mouse bursting out of a wall, scavenging for cheese-flavored chips; a third has a young woman falling over because she's looking at her chips and not the road. All five of the finalists contain the same predictable, dorm-room aesthetic, low production qualities, and poor acting. The brain trust at Doritos deserves thanks for not exposing us to the other 1,100 entrants.

Intrinsic Talent

Why is the work of the amateur of a lesser quality than professionally made content? There's the intrinsic talent of a lifelong professional, such as Ridley Scott, of course. Then there's the financial resource made available to the professional content creator. Back in 1984, Apple paid Chast/Day $1.6 million to produce their Mac ad. Today, according to the American Association of Advertising Agencies, the average professionally produced 30-second spot costs $381,000. In contrast, wedding photographer Jarod Cicon, one of the five finalists in the Doritos competition, estimates that his 30-second ad cost $150 to produce.

Web 2.0 advocates, who are apologists for user-generated content (such as Chris Anderson, the author of the best-selling book *The Long Tail*), promise that the amateurs of the new digital democracy can create the same quality content for a tiny proportion of the traditional cost. But this simply isn't true. Watch the Doritos commercials side-by-side with some classic Super Bowl commercials, such as the Budweiser "Frogs" (1995) or "Cedric" (2001) spots. It's like tasting a homemade elderberry wine after a glass of the best Cabernet.

The economics of amateur hour at the Super Bowl are disturbing. If today's typical commercial costs $381,000 and an amateur advertisement costs $150 to produce, then what happens to the money which isn't spent on the creative? Given that Doritos are awarding $10,000 to the five finalists in their talent show, that still leaves some $331,000 on the table. To use a fashionable Web 2.0 term, the professional creator is being "disintermediated." CBS doesn't lose anything because they still charge Doritos over $2.5 million for the 30 second spot. Instead, it's the professional creator—the scriptwriter, cameraman, audio expert—who is being squeezed out of the economy by this infestation of amateur content.

Worse, not Better

Markets are markets and there's no reason to cry for simply for the loss of jobs in one sector, so long as new efficiencies are being created. But in this instance, the loss of jobs is accompanied by *worse*, not better products. This is true across the media industry and not just in the advertising business.

As Columbia University economics professor Jagwish Bhagwati has argued, digital technology is undermining the wages of the American middle class. Web 2.0 technologies which enable amateurs to make dumbed-down replicas of professional work are particularly responsible for what Bhagwati calls the "tsumani" of downward pressure on wages created by new technology.

Amateur content on user-generated video sites such as Google's YouTube is undermining the value of professionally made video content. *American Idol* now has an online competition called "American Idol Underground," which is making the traditional music A&R [artist and repertoire] person redundant. [Publisher] Harper Collins is undermining the traditional role of literary agents by running online competitions to "discover" amateur writers. The result of all this democratization of media is fewer creative jobs and more amateurish books, movies, and music. And commercials, too.

13

User-Generated Content Does Not Threaten Advertising

Joe Marchese

Joe Marchese is president of Archetype Media, a Southern California–based advertising agency that specializes in social media.

Although advertisements showcasing user-generated content have surfaced in high-profile campaigns to much fanfare, advertising agencies and industry professionals will not take a backseat to Webcam-wielding amateurs in the foreseeable future. In fact, the term "user-generated advertising" is misleading because it downplays the submissions, review, and selection processes that advertisers control when user-generated content is featured in advertising campaigns. Furthermore, contests and projects calling for advertisements by amateurs are akin to talent searches and may become crowded with competitors from small production companies and independent agencies instead of consumers.

User-generated advertising is not the future of advertising. The task of imagining, producing and distributing a compelling brand message will not be left to whoever chooses to pick up a webcam on a random Sunday afternoon. Instead, I propose that the radical shift, commonly mis-titled user-generated advertising, descending over the world of advertising is in fact better called *distributed creative development* (couldn't find the term on a Google search, so let's coin it on the [advertising industry Web site online] Spin).

If you were at OMMA Hollywood last week [the Online Media, Marketing, and Advertising Expo, March 2007], you were no doubt inspired (or worried) by the success story of Doritos' "user-generated" Super Bowl commercial and feel-good story surrounding the teams that produced the winning spots. But if you watched the presentation, you would have seen that there was a significant coordinated effort to establish and promote the contest—including developing the technology platform for participation, the operations for submission review, and numerous other moving pieces that had to work in perfect unison. The coordinated achievement incorporated the efforts of Doritos' creative agency, PR, media buying, among other partners. There was direction given to the participants, similar to the direction a brand might give any agency pre-pitch. In the end, it was not a "set it and forget it" solution, it was a carefully, and might I add artfully, managed process.

One of the winning teams was present to receive Doritos Managing Director Jason McDonell's glowing endorsement for future work from the advertisers in the audience. I don't think I missed the stipulation that the winning team had to be users of whatever product was going to approach them for work. I am sure they would have been open to work from a number of brands. Wouldn't that make them a talented creative/production group looking to make a profession of advertising, not a "user"? In fact, that's, exactly what they are.

An Open Call

The truth is that many entrants in these types of contests (advertising, video, music etc.) are aspiring professionals, or at least hobbyists approaching amateur status. For this reason, "user"-generated advertising contests can demonstrate many characteristics similar to an open call for creative development. In this open call the prize money plus the perceived value of recognition is the total compensation. It is for this reason that the Doritos Super Bowl commercial contest more closely mirrored "American Idol" than a karaoke contest. Raise your hand if you think "American Idol" is user-generated content, or the contestants are your everyday kids (never mind—I can't see you anyway). "American Idol" is a talent search, judged by the people the talent is supposed to affect—a better comparison for distributed creative development.

It's easy to see why agencies not looking for the recognition, which would be most established agencies, could not justify the expense of participating in the contest against its expected financial outcome. But what about when marketers increasingly turn to distributed creative development? There are a number of market effects that will have to play out. Doritos had the market to itself in many ways for this run. All of the press clips that Doritos showed (read: free promotion of its contest and its spot) won't occur the sixth and seventh time "users" get their ad distributed on a major platform. Also, the more brands that test the market for distributed creative development, the greater the demand for amateurs' and aspiring professionals' time. This will drive up the cost of attracting the critical mass of submissions (the key to reducing the risk of distributed creative development). Will the cost get high enough that we will see smaller interactive and independent agencies participating in these open calls? Can you create an efficient market for distributed creative development (Google, are you listening?)

As the market determines a price, and all hidden costs and risks are assessed for distributed creative development, traditional full-service agencies will be forced to compete against the cost of initiating, managing and compensating a successful distributed creative campaign. Traditional agencies will also have to match the success rate of distributed creative development.

Successful agencies will adapt to be able to participate in a market with elements of distributed creative development.

This will take three forms: 1) facilitating or providing complementary services; 2) leveraging expertise and adapting organization to actually participate efficiently in the market of open calls for creative; and 3) utilizing advances in technology to consistently outperform cost and effectiveness measurements of the distributed creative market (and being able to prove it). Don't say this isn't possible; look at the funds that consistently outperform financial markets. So who is Madison Avenue's [investment bank giant] Goldman Sachs?

Organizations to Contact

The editors have compiled the following list of organizations concerned with the issues debated in this book. The descriptions are derived from materials provided by the organizations. All have publications or information available for interested readers. The list was compiled on the date of publication of the present volume; the information provided here may change. Be aware that many organizations take several weeks or longer to respond to inquiries, so allow as much time as possible.

Association of Music Podcasting
e-mail: info@musicpodcasting.org
Web site: www.musicpodcasting.org

The Association of Music Podcasting (AMP) is a membership group of music podcasters who wish to promote and support the podcasting medium. All members of AMP have regular podcasts that have been judged by their peers to maintain a high standard of quality. As part of its mission, AMP wishes to work not only with music podcasters, but also with the artists who provide podsafe music to the public. The association also supports listeners by offering not only a list of quality podcasts, but also a podcast that is a distillation of many member shows.

Center for Democracy and Technology
1634 Eye Street, NW #1100, Washington, DC   20006
(202) 637-9800 • fax: (202) 637-0968
e-mail: info@cdt.org
Web site: www.cdt.org

The Center for Democracy and Technology's (CDT) mission is to develop public policy solutions that advance constitutional civil liberties and democratic values in new computer and communications media. Pursuing its mission through policy research, public education, and coalition building, CDT works to increase citizens' privacy and the public's control over the use of personal information held by government and other institutions. Its publications include issue briefs, policy papers, and *CDT Policy Posts*, an online, occasional publication that covers issues regarding the civil liberties of those using the information highway.

Digital Video Professionals Association

135 Interstate Boulevard, Ste. One, Greenville, SC   29615
(888) 339-DVPA (3872) • fax: (864) 286-6229
e-mail: info@dvpa.com
Web site: www.dvpa.com

The Digital Video Professionals Association (DVPA) is an international community of new media professionals that provides membership to all those who are involved as visual communicators using digital media. This includes, but is not limited to, producers, directors, educators, animators, videographers, editors, motion graphic artists, film groups, production managers, video game developers, advertising agencies, television stations, and design studios.

Electronic Frontier Foundation

454 Shotwell Street, San Francisco, CA   94110-1914
(415) 436-9333 • fax: (415) 436-9993
e-mail: eff@eff.org
Web site: www.eff.org

Electronic Frontier Foundation (EFF) is an organization of students and other individuals that aims to promote a better understanding of telecommunications issues. It fosters awareness of civil liberties issues arising from advancements in computer-based communications media and supports litigation to preserve, protect, and extend First Amendment rights in computing and telecommunications technologies. EFF's publications include *Building the Open Road, Crime and Puzzlement,* the quarterly newsletter *Networks & Policy,* the bi-weekly electronic newsletter *EFFector Online,* and online bulletins and publications, including *First Amendment in Cyberspace.*

Integrated Media Association

PO Box 810, Rhinebeck, NY   12572

(845) 876-2577 • fax: (845) 876-2578

Web site: www.integratedmedia.org

Integrated Media Association (IMA), formerly known as the Public Radio Internet Station Alliance (PRISA), aims to help public broadcasters benefit from the Internet and other forms of new media. Through its meetings, conferences, collaborative projects and publications, IMA continues to provide a center within public broadcasting for online service information, policy, and practice.

Internet Society

1775 Wiehle Ave., Ste. 102, Reston, VA   20190-5108

(703) 326-9880 • fax: (703) 326-9881

e-mail isoc@isoc.org

Web site: www.isoc.org

The Internet Society (ISOC) is a group of technologists, developers, educators, researchers, government representatives, and businesspeople. The Society supports the development and dissemination of standards for the Internet and works to ensure global cooperation and coordination for the Internet and related Internet-working technologies and applications. It publishes the bimonthly magazine *On the Internet.*

Media Bloggers Association

(928) 223-5711

e-mail: info@mediabloggers.org

Web site: www.mediabloggers.org

The Media Bloggers Association (MBA) is a non-partisan organization dedicated to promoting, protecting, and educating its members; supporting the development of "blogging" or "citizen journalism" as a distinct form of media; and helping to extend the power of the press, with all the rights and responsibilities that entails, to every citizen.

The Online News Association
PO Box 2022, New York, NY   10101-2022
(646) 290-7900
e-mail: lschwab@journalists.org
Web site: www.journalists.org

The Online News Association (ONA) is composed largely of professional online journalists. ONA has more than 1,000 professional members—people whose principal livelihood involves gathering or producing news for digital presentation. The membership includes news writers, producers, designers, editors, photographers, and others who produce news for the Internet or other digital delivery systems, as well as academic members and others interested in the development of online journalism.

Ultimate Podcast Alliance and Consortium
12404 Radnor Lane, Second Floor, Laurel, MD   20708
e-mail: webmaster@upaac.org
Web site: www.upaac.org

The Ultimate Podcast Alliance and Consortium (UPAAC) is a membership organization that focuses on creating opportunity for development of multimedia content on the Internet. It is a clearinghouse and resource center for tools, knowledge, and other resources related to the development of podcasting as the future of radio, television, and entertainment generally.

U.S. Copyright Office
101 Independence Ave., SE, Washington, DC   20559-6000
(202) 707-5959
Web site: www.copyright.gov

The U.S. Copyright Office provides expert assistance to Congress on intellectual property matters; advises Congress on anticipated changes in U.S. copyright law; analyzes and assists in drafting copyright legislation and legislative reports, and provides and undertakes studies for Congress; and offers advice to Congress on compliance with multilateral agreements.

Bibliography

Books

Dennis Cooper, ed. — *The Userlands: New Fiction from the Blogging Underground.* New York: Akashic Books, 2007.

Anja Ebersbach, Markus Glaser, and Richard Heigl — *Wiki: Web Collaboration.* New York: Springer, 2005.

Jack Goldsmith and Tim Wu — *Who Controls the Internet?: Illusions of a Borderless World.* New York: Oxford University Press, 2006.

Lawrence Lessig — *The Future of Ideas: The Fate of the Commons in a Connected World.* New York: Random House, 2001.

Jay Liebowitz — *Social Networking: The Essence of Innovation.* Lanham, MD: Scarecrow Press, 2007.

J. R. Okin — *The Information Revolution: The Not-for-Dummies Guide to the History, Technology, and Use of the World Wide Web.* Winter Harbor, ME: Ironbound Press, 2005.

Howard Rheingold — *Smart Mobs: The Next Social Revolution.* Cambridge, MA: Basic Books, 2003.

Will Richardson — *Blogs, Wikis, Podcasts, and Other Powerful Web Tools for Classrooms.* Thousand Oaks, CA: Corwin Press, 2006.

Robert Scoble and Shel Israel
Naked Conversations: How Blogs Are Changing the Way Businesses Talk with Customers. Hoboken, NJ: John Wiley & Sons, 2006.

Don Tapscott and Anthony D. Williams
Wikinomics: How Mass Collaboration Changes Everything. New York: Portfolio, 2006.

David Weinberger
Everything Is Miscellaneous: The Power of the New Digital Disorder. New York: Times Books, 2007.

Jonathan Yang
The Rough Guide to Blogging. New York: Penguin Group, 2006.

Periodicals

Associated Press
"TV Networks and Advertisers Increasingly Capitalize on Viewer-Created Content," March 10, 2007.

Paula Berinstein
"Wikipedia and Britannica: The Kid's All Right (and So Is the Old Man)," *Searcher*, March 2006.

George Catlin
"Online Videos May Not Be as 'Viral' as You Think," *Hartford Courant*, September 2, 2006.

Doug Chandler
"Web 2.0: Buzzword or Bonanza?" *Electric Wholesaling*, May 1, 2007.

Jeremy Clarkson
"The End Is Nigh, See it on YouTube," *Sunday Times* (UK), January 28, 2007.

Chris DeWolf   "The MySpace Generation," *Forbes*, May 7, 2007.

Jan Farrington   "On-Line Friendships: How They Touch Your Real-Life World," *Current Health 2*, April–May 2007.

Viv Groskop   "Internet Killed the Video Star," *New Statesman*, July 10, 2006.

Lev Grossman   "*Time*'s Person of the Year: You," *Time*, December 31, 2006.

James Hebert   "Podcasting? Relax, It's a Piece of Cake," *San Diego Union-Tribune*, September 18, 2005.

Catherine Holahan   "The Web, Now Just for You," *Business Week*, February 9, 2007.

Gregory Lamb   "Online Wikipedia Is Not Britannica—But It's Close," *Christian Science Monitor*, January 5, 2006.

Kevin Maney   "2006 May Be the Year of 'You,' but 2007 May Be the Year to Get Over It," *USA Today*, December 19, 2006.

Bill Mitchell   "Weblogs: A Road Back to Basics," *Neiman Reports*, Fall 2003.

Kim Peterson   "Video Revolution Comes to the Computer Screen," *Seattle Times*, October 2, 2006.

Alex Pham   "Social Network Website Reaches a Hire Level," *Los Angeles Times*, May 7, 2007.

Maria Puente	"Get an Earful of Offbeat Podcasts," *USA Today*, March 15, 2007.
George Raine	"It's Not a Passing Fad: In YouTube Era, More Superbowl Ads and Themes Are Coming from Amateurs," *San Francisco Chronicle*, January 28, 2007.
Phil Rosenthal	"Reporting from the Scene, Witnesses Act as Journalists," *Chicago Tribune*, April 17, 2007.
Ken Schachter	"Golden User-Generated Opportunity," *Red Herring*, May 9, 2007.
Dan Schmit	"Creating a Podcast Empire . . . From the Corner of Your Classroom!" *Multimedia & Internet@Schools*, January–February 2007.
Nikki Schwab and Sean Dustman	"The World of Military Blogging," *Washington Post*, May 3, 2007.
Michelle Slatalla	"Online Worlds Give Kids a Chance to Run Their Own Show," *New York Times*, May 6, 2007.
Raymond Snoddy	"Raymond Snoddy on Media: User Content Won't Kill Off Old Media," *Marketing*, January 17, 2007.
Catherine Taylor	"When Will Viral Become Viable? Web Video Has Redefined Our Culture, but a Profitable Model Remains Elusive," *ADWEEK*, November 27, 2006.

Index

A

Acuff-Rose Music Inc., Campbell v.
(1994), 82
Ad sales, on social networking
sites, 69–70
Adobe Flash Player, 74
Advertising
user-generated content does
not threaten, 95–98
user-generated content threat-
ens, 91–94
AirTroductions, 64
Allbritton, Christopher, 44
Allen, Gracie, 88
Aloneness, 19–20
Amateur filmmaking, 75–76
See also Viral videos
American Heartbreak, 87
American Idol, 94, 97
Anderson, Chris, 93
Anderson, Tom, 11, 16, 19, 60
Appell, David, 44
Attention needs, 61–62
Authentic media, 8

B

Back-to-Iraq.com, 44
Bands, 16, 87–88
Bauer, John, 62–63
BBC, 25
BellSouth, 33
Berners-Lee, Tim, 59
Bhagwati, Jagwish, 94
Blip.tv, 74–75
Block, Michael, 58, 61

Blogs/blogging
importance of, to journalism,
35–46
is not journalism, 47–56
as mosaic of everyday life,
55–56
obscurity of most, 22
popularity of, 37
proliferation of, 12
truth and, 54–55
Boud, Daniel, 58
Britannica, Wikipedia vs., 27–30
Broadband connections, 26, 59–
60, 74
Browning, Randy, 60
Burns, George, 88
Butler, Michael, 87
Buzz, 23
Buzznet, 60

C

Campbell v. Acuff-Rose Music Inc.
(1994), 82
Cauz, Jorge, 29
Chen, Steve, 13
Chiat/Day, 92, 93
Chinese language, 12
Clear Channel, 89
Coldplay, 36
Collaborative content, 13–14
Collective sites, 13–14
Communications Decency Act, 33
Community, fostered by blogs,
45–46